Raven's Call

A Quaint and Curious Anthology of Forgotten Lore

About the Author

Raven Grimassi (1951-2019) was a prolific occult author who had written more than twenty books on various magical, pagan, and occult topics. He is best known for his work in popularizing the branch of Italian witchcraft known as Stregheria and was an active member of the pagan community for decades. He is survived by not only his books, but also his loving wife Stephanie who continues to make magic in his name.

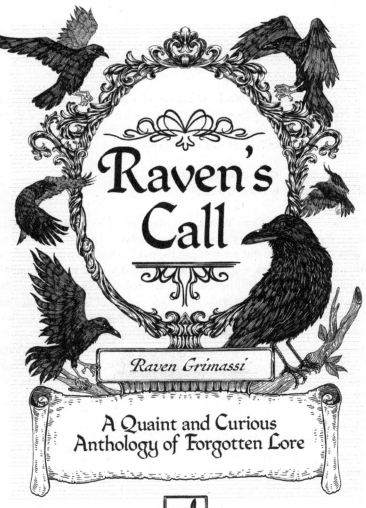

Raven's Call

Raven Grimassi

A Quaint and Curious Anthology of Forgotten Lore

Chicago, IL

Raven's Call © 2025 by Raven Grimassi. All rights reserved. No part of this book may be reproduced in any manner whatsoever without written permission from Crossed Crow Books, except in the case of brief quotations embodied in critical articles and reviews.

Paperback ISBN: 978-1-964537-12-2
Library of Congress Control Number on file.

Disclaimer: Crossed Crow Books, LLC does not participate in, endorse, or have any authority or responsibility concerning private business transactions between our authors and the public. Any internet references contained in this work were found to be valid during the time of publication, however, the publisher cannot guarantee that a specific reference will continue to be maintained. This book's material is not intended to diagnose, treat, cure, or prevent any disease, disorder, ailment, or any physical or psychological condition. The author, publisher, and its associates shall not be held liable for the reader's choices when approaching this book's material. The views and opinions expressed within this book are those of the author alone and do not necessarily reflect the views and opinions of the publisher.

Published by:
Crossed Crow Books, LLC
518 Davis St, Suite 205
Evanston, IL 60201
www.crossedcrowbooks.com

Printed in the United States of America.
IBI

Other Books from Raven Grimassi

*Instruments of the Craft:
Mastering the Four Tools of the Witch*

*Crafting a Tradition of Witchcraft: Building a
Foundation for Your Magical Beliefs & Practices*

Witchcraft: A Mystery Tradition

*Cauldron of Memory: Retrieving Ancestral
Knowledge and Wisdom*

*The Witches' Craft: The Roots of Witchcraft
& Magical Transformation*

Wiccan Magick: Inner Teachings of the Craft

Wiccan Mysteries: Ancient Origins & Teachings

Table of Contents

Wiccan Aspects and Leland's Italian Witchcraft 1

The Celebration of May 13

Honoring Ancestral Spirits 19

The Witches' Circle 23

The Rites of Summer 27

The Mystery Tradition Within Wicca 31

Exploring the Legend of the Descent of the Goddess . 37

The Tarot Magician: An Occult Tradition 43

The Full Moon in Witchcraft Rituals 47

Working with Magick Mirrors 55

Spell of the Witches' Ring 61

Italian Witchcraft: The Survival of a Tradition 65

The Veglia, Sacred Fire, and Italian Witchcraft 75

Lupercus: Wolf God of Winter 83

The Saturnalia 89

The Benandanti 93

The Spirit Blade 97

The Stag & The Wolf 101

Mama Strega's Spellbook 109

Select Articles from Moon Shadow

Walnut Witches 115

The Triad Traditions 117

Witchcraft in Tuscany 119

The Watchers: Secrets of the Tanarric Witches 125

Herbs of the Old Religion 131

The Gesture of Power 135

The Cimaruta 137

The Spirits of Italy... 139

The Divine King: The Slain God................................. 147

Aradia and the Witches 153

The Spirit Flame.. 157

The Rite of Union 161

The Nanta Bag... 163

The Fava Bean.. 167

Bibliography... 171

Note from the Editor

Raven's Call was a periodical produced and distributed by Raven Grimassi in the early 2000s. The periodical featured articles written by Raven as well as other occultists and witches in the community. What follows is a curated and edited compilation of Grimassi's contributions to the magazine.

Like every practitioner, Raven's thoughts and practice changed throughout his life. With every article, the reader travels through time, witnessing his evolving ideas and his steadfast dedication to the Craft.

While *Raven's Call* was not widely distributed, the magazine still left its mark on those who were fortunate enough to read it. We are incredibly grateful to his wife, Stephanie Grimassi, for making these works available, and we are honored at Crossed Crow Books to share his work with the wider community.

Wiccan Aspects and Leland's Italian Witchcraft

Many people today believe that various concepts associated with Wicca such as skyclad worship, cakes and wine celebrations, and the worship of a male and female deity originated with Gerald Gardner's writings on Wicca circa 1954. These and many other aspects seen in modern Wicca are often pointed to as specific "Gardnerian markers" that "prove" traditions to be evolved from Gardnerian Wicca. In this article, we will explore the foundations of these basic tenets found in modern Wicca, comparing them with aspects of Italian Witchcraft as it was defined at the close of the nineteenth century. Without exception, we will find that there exists no single basic element of modern Wicca (as defined by Gardner) that is not predated in the writings of Charles Godfrey Leland on Italian Witchcraft over half a century earlier. Leland was a folklorist who investigated Witchcraft in Italy from 1892–1899, claiming to have made direct contact with a surviving tradition.

In Gardner's book *Witchcraft Today*, he introduces the reader to the word *wicca*, a theme he expands upon in his book *The*

Raven's Call

Meaning of Witchcraft. Gardner claims that wicca is the root word for *Witchcraft*. In Chapter Four of Leland's book *Gypsy Sorcery & Fortune Telling*, Leland earlier presented the following: *"As for the English word Witch, Anglo-Saxon Wicca, comes from a root implying wisdom..."* [1]

Leland's footnote here reads: *"Witch: Mediaeval English wicche, both masculine and feminine, a wizard, a Witch. Anglo-Saxon wicca, masculine, wicce, feminine. Wicca is a corruption of witga, commonly used as a short form of witega, a prophet, seer, magician, or sorcerer. Anglo-Saxon witan, to see, allied to witan, to know..."* [2]

In the introduction to *Etruscan Roman Remains in Popular Tradition*, Leland writes: *"Among these people, stregeria, or Witchcraft—or, as I have heard it called, "la vecchia religione' (or the 'old religion')—exists to a degree which would even astonish many Italians."* [3]

Leland speaks further of Italian Witchcraft as a religion in his book *Aradia: Gospel of the Witches*. In the appendix, we read: *"The result of it all was a vast development of rebels, outcasts, and all the discontented, who adopted Witchcraft or sorcery for a religion, and wizards as their priests. They had secret meetings in desert places, among old ruins accursed by priests as the haunt of evil spirits or ancient heathen gods, or in the mountains. To this day the dweller in Italy may often find secluded spots environed by ancient chestnut forests, rocks, and walls,*

---

1 Charles Godfrey Leland, *Gypsy Sorcery and Fortune Telling* (*Charles Scribner's Sons*, 1891) 66.

2 Ibid.

3 Charles Godrey Leland, *Etruscan Roman Remains in Popular Tradition* (C. Scribner's Sons, 1892) 2.

Wiccan Aspects and Leland's Italian Witchcraft

which suggest fit places for the Sabbat, and are sometimes still believed by tradition to be such." [4]

The gathering of Witches beneath the Full Moon is seen by some as another modern indicator of Gardnerian Wiccan practice. However, we find several references to it in Leland's work, particularly in *Aradia: Gospel of the Witches*, where Leland gives an account of the following words to be spoken during a ritual:

> *"When I shall have departed from this world,*
> *Whenever ye have need of anything,*
> *Once in the month, and when the Moon is full,*
> *Ye shall assemble in some desert place,*
> *Or in a forest all together join*
> *To adore the potent spirit of your queen,*
> *My mother, great Diana. She who fain*
> *Would learn all sorcery yet has not won*
> *Its deepest secrets, then my mother will*
> *Teach her, in truth all things as yet unknown."* [5]

During the rites of Witchcraft, Leland describes a ceremonial celebration that includes cakes and wine. This is another aspect commonly attributed to the structure of Gardnerian Wicca. In

---

4 Charles Godfrey Leland, "Appendix: Comments on the Foregoing Texts" in *Aradia: Gospel of the Witches* (David Nutt, 1899). https://sacred-texts.com/pag/aradia/ara18.htm.

5 Charles Godfrey Leland, "How Diana Gave Birth to Aradia (Herodias)" in *Aradia: Gospel of the Witches* (David Nutt, 1899). http://sacred-texts.com/pag/aradia/ara03.htm.

Leland's Aradia, we read several references: *"The supper of the Witches, the cakes of meal, salt, and honey, in the form of crescent Moons, are known to every classical scholar. The Moon or horn shaped cakes are still common. I have eaten of them to this very day, and though they are known all over the world, I believe they owe their fashion to tradition."* [6]

"You shall make cakes of meal, wine, salt, and honey in the shape of a (crescent or horned) Moon, and then put them to bake…"

"And thus shall it be done: all shall sit down to the supper all naked, men and women, and the feast over, they shall dance, sing, make music…"

"O Diana!
In honor of thee I will hold this feast,
Feast and drain the goblet deep,
We will dance and wildly leap…" [7]

Leland goes on to write about the custom of being naked during the Full Moon ceremony. Gardner spoke of ritual nudity, giving it the term *skyclad*. Again, many modern Witches believe this ritual nudity originated with Gerald Gardner. However, in Leland's Aradia, we read two distinct passages related to ritual nudity: *"And so ye shall be free in everything; And as the sign that ye are truly free, Ye shall be naked in your rites, both men and women also…"*

---

6   Charles Godfrey Leland, "Appendix: Comments on the Foregoing Texts" in *Aradia: Gospel of the Witches* (David Nutt, 1899). https://sacred-texts.com/pag/aradia/ara18.htm.

7   Charles Godfrey Leland, "The Sabbat: Treguenda or Witch-Meeting— How to Consecrate the Supper" in *Aradia: Gospel of the Witches* (David Nutt, 1899). https//sacred-texts.com/pag/aradia/ara04.htm.

Wiccan Aspects and Leland's Italian Witchcraft

"And thus shall it be done: all shall sit down to the supper all naked, men and women, and the feast over; they shall dance, sing, make music..." [8]

Leland goes on to present a God and Goddess mythos. Here, he writes of the Roman deities Diana (goddess of the Moon) and Lucifer (the herald of light) as being worshipped by Witches. He recounts: *"Diana was the first created before all creation; in her were all things; out of herself, the first darkness, she divided herself; into darkness and light she was divided. Lucifer, her brother and son, herself and her other half, was the light."*

"Lucifer was extremely angry; but Diana with her wiles of Witchcraft so charmed him that he yielded to her love. This was the first fascination; she hummed the song, it was as the buzzing of bees (or a top spinning round), a spinning-wheel spinning life. She spun the lives of all men; all things were spun from the wheel of Diana. Lucifer turned the wheel." [9]

In Chapter Nine, Leland writes: *"The ancient myth is, to begin with, one of darkness and light, or day and night, from which are born the fifty-one (now fifty-two) weeks of the year. This is Diana, the night, and Apollo, the sun or light in another form..."* [10]

---

8   Charles Godfrey Leland, "How Diana Gave Birth to Aradia (Herodias)" in *Aradia: Gospel of the Witches* (David Knutt, 1899). https://sacred-texts.com/pag/aradia/ara03.htm.

9   Charles Godfrey Leland, "How Diana Made the Stars and the Rain" in *Aradia: Gospel of the Witches* (David Knutt, 1899). https//sacred-texts.com/pag/aradia/ara05.htm.

10 Charles Godfrey Leland, "Tana and Endamone, or Diana and Endymion" in *Aradia: Gospel of the Witches* (David Knutt, 1899). https://sacred-texts.com/pag/aradia/ara11.htm.

And in the Appendix, we find: *"Now be it observed that every leading point which forms the plot or center of this Vangelo, such as that Diana is Queen of the Witches; an associate of Herodius (Aradia) in her relations to sorcery; that she bore a child to her brother the Sun (here Lucifer); that as a Moon-goddess she is..."* [11]

The theme of a male and female deity worshipped by Witches appears in several of Leland's works on Italian Witchcraft, such as *Legends of Florence*. However, Leland's main focus regarding the Witches' deity is focused upon Diana. In Chapter Four, Leland gives one of the Witches' prayers:

> *"Diana, beautiful Diana!*
> *Who art indeed as good as beautiful,*
> *By all the worship I have given thee,*
> *And all the joy of love which thou hast known,*
> *I do implore thee..."* [12]

In Chapter Ten, he recounts the words of Aradia to her Witches: *"Why worship a deity whom you cannot see, when there is the Moon in all her splendor visible? Worship her. Invoke Diana, the goddess of the Moon, and she will grant your prayers. This shalt thou do, obeying the Gospel of (the Witches and of) Diana, who is Queen of the Fairies and the Moon."* [13]

---

11 Charles Godfrey Leland, "Appendix: Comments on the Foregoing Texts" in *Aradia: Gospel of the Witches* (David Knutt, 1899). https://sacred-texts.com/pag/aradia/ara18.htm.

12 Charles Godfrey Leland, "The Charm of the Stones Consecrated to Diana" in *Aradia: Gospel of the Witches* (David Knutt, 1899). https://sacred-texts.com/pag/aradia/ara06.htm.

13 Charles Godfrey Leland, "Madonna Diana" in *Aradia: Gospel of the Witches* (David Knutt, 1899). https://sacred-texts.com/pag/aradia/ara12.htm

Wiccan Aspects and Leland's Italian Witchcraft

In modern Wicca, a spiritual race known as the Watchers is another of the so-called Gardnerian markers. Their notation in Leland's material is apparent only when one examines the ancient Italic evidence related to guardian spirits and then looks at Leland's references. In the book *Archaic Roman Religion* by George Dumezil, we find that guardian spirits known as Lares were worshipped at the crossroads where small towers were erected. An altar was set in front of the towers, and offerings were given to them.[14] This is not unlike the Watchtowers of Gardnerian Wicca. The Lares were originally nature spirits of the fields, derived from the Etruscan lasa spirit. Later, they became spirits of demarcation associated with protection and seasonal rites.

In the ancient stellar Cults of Mesopotamia, later imported into Rome, there were four "royal" stars called the "Watchers." Each one of these stars ruled over one of the four cardinal points common to astrology. The star Aldebaran, when it marked the spring equinox, held the position of "Watcher" of the East. Regulus, marking the summer solstice, was "Watcher" of the South. Antares, marking the autumn equinox, was "Watcher" of the West. Fomalhaut, marking the winter solstice, was "Watcher" of the North. Here, we have the connections of the term "watchers" with the stars. This is noted and discussed in two books titled *The Lure of the Heavens: A History of Astrology* by Donald Papon and *Star Names: Their lore and Meaning* by Richard Allen.

In Charles Leland's *Aradia*, he recounts the tale of the "Children of Diana, or how the fairies were born" in which Diana created *"the great spirits of the stars."* As we have seen, the great spirits or rulers of the stars are known as Watchers. Leland also

---

14 George Dumezil, *Archaic Roman Religion* (John Hopkins University Press, 1996) 343–344.

writes of the elder race: *"Then Diana went to the Fathers of the Beginning, to the Mothers, the Spirits who were before the first spirit, and lamented unto them that she could not prevail with Lucifer. And they praised her for her courage; they told her that to rise she must fall; to become the chief of goddesses she must become a mortal."* [15]

In some modern traditions of Witchcraft, the Watchers are also known as spirits of the Four Elements. Leland refers to Elemental spirits in the introduction of his book *Etruscan Romain Remains*, where he writes: *"Closely allied to the belief in these old deities, is a vast mass of curious traditions, such as that there is a spirit of every element."* [16]

In Gardner's works, he deals with the topic of formal initiation into the Old Religion of the Witches. Leland refers to initiation in Chapter Ten of *Etruscan Roman Remains: "As for families in which stregheria, or a knowledge of charms, old traditions and songs is preserved…as the children grow older, if any aptitude is observed in them for sorcery, some old grandmother or aunt takes them in hand, and initiates them into the ancient faith."* [17]

In certain Gardnerian verses, particularly those often credited to Doreen Valiente, we find a link between initiation and reincarnation. In such verses, the recurrent theme is that one must be born anew, meet again, and remember those who were loved before.

---

15 Charles Godfrey Leland, "How Diana Made the Stars and the Rain" in *Aradia: Gospel of the Witches* (David Knutt, 1899). https://sacred-texts.com/pag/aradia/ara05.htm

16 Charles Godfrey Leland, "Etruscan Roman Remains in Popular Tradition" in *Aradia: Gospel of the Witches (*David Knutt, 1899). https://www.sacred-texts.com/pag/err/err13.htm.

17 Ibid.

Leland addresses reincarnation in several chapters of his book *Etruscan Roman Remains*. In the introduction, he writes: *"...also that sorcerers and Witches are sometimes born again in their descendants."* [18]

In Chapter Ten, he writes: *"It is also believed in the Romagna that those who are specially of the strega faith die, but reappear again in human forms. This is a rather obscure esoteric doctrine, known in the Witch families but not much talked about. A child is born, when, after due family consultation some very old and wise strega detects in it a long-departed grandfather by his smile, features, or expression."* [19]

Leland continues: *"Dr. O. W. HOLMES has shrewdly observed that when a child is born, some person old enough to have triangulated the descent, can recognise very often the grandparent or great-uncle in the descendant. In the Witch families, who cling together and intermarry, these triangulations lead to more frequent discoveries of palingenesis than in others. In one of the strange stories in this book relating to Benevento, a father is born again as his own child, and then marries his second mother. But the spirit of the departed wizard has at times certainly some choice in the matter, and he occasionally elects to be born again as a nobleman or prince."* [20]

He finally concludes: *"In this we may trace the process by which the Witch or sorcerer, by being re-born, becomes more powerful, and passes to the higher stage of a spirit."* [21]

---

18   Ibid.
19   Ibid
20   Ibid.
21   Ibid.

We have looked at many topics in this article: use of the term the Old Religion, Full Moon ritual, cakes and wine celebration, ritual nudity, God and Goddess worship, the Watchers, initiation, reincarnation, and Elementals. As we saw, these aspects appear in Leland's work over half a century earlier than the writings of Gerald Gardner on these same topics. Despite the documented chronology clearly demonstrating that these aspects all appear in Italian Witchcraft as late as 1899, many commentators cling to the belief that the inclusion of each of these topics within a tradition is a certain sign of Gardnerian influence.

Gardner's books were primarily responsible for launching the Wiccan movement as we now know it. The major attention of the Craft Community had long been focused on the related writings by Doreen Valiente, Ray Buckland, and others. This interest brought forth an abundance of Celtic traditions, and—in time—many people came to simply accept that all the tenets, rites, and practices originated with Gardnerian Wicca. However, just because Gardner, and those of his lineage, popularized such material does not mean that such things did not preexist elsewhere. Publishing something first does not necessarily equate with inventing it or having a market on it.

It is clear from Gardner and his associates' writings that various materials and cultural aspects were incorporated into Gardnerian Wicca. In the early days, Doreen Valiente can be included among those who contributed various ritual poems, verses, and concepts. In *Witchcraft Today* and *The Meaning of Witchcraft,* Gardner writes of his visits to Italy and of his interests in Roman Paganism. He notes similarities between Wiccan practices and scenes depicted in the murals at Pompeii. He also mentions the similarities between

Wiccan Aspects and Leland's Italian Witchcraft

ancient Roman Mystery Cults and modern Wiccan concepts. From his comments, we can be sure that Gardner was studying Roman Paganism while he was writing about Wicca.

Doreen Valiente readily admitted that the writings of Charles Leland on Italian Witchcraft first drew her to the Old Religion. The well-known version of the *Charge of the Goddess* written by Valiente contains verses almost identical to Leland's earlier Italian version. Aleister Crowley spent several years in Sicily studying and practicing occultism. Everywhere one looks at Gardnerian Wicca and the writings of its early initiates, one can find a connection to Italy. Perhaps one day the influence of Leland's writings on the development of modern Wicca might even be acknowledged.

The Celebration of May

May Day celebrations are a time to acknowledge the return of growth and the end of decline within the cycle of life. The rites of May are rooted in ancient fertility festivals that can be traced back to the Great Mother festivals of the Hellenistic period of Greco-Roman religion. The ancient festival of Floralia culminated on May 1st with offerings of flowers and garlands to the Roman goddesses Flora and Maia. The month of May is named for the goddess Maia.

In 1724, the noted occultist Dr. William Stukeley, in his work titled the *Itinerarium Curiosum*, describes a maypole near Horn Castle, Lincolnshire, that reportedly stood on the site of a former Roman *herms* (a wood or stone carving of a human upper torso emerging from a pillar). The author records that boys *"annually keep up the festival of the Floralia on May Day"* and carried white willow wands covered with cowslips. Stukeley goes on to say that these wands are derived from the thyrsus wands once carried in the ancient Roman Bacchanal rites.[22]

May festivals commonly incorporate elements of pre-Christian worship related to agricultural themes. In ancient times, a young

---

22 W. C. Hazlitt, *Dictionary of Faiths & Folklore* (Bracken Books, 1995) 402–406.

male was chosen to symbolize the spirit of the plant kingdom, known by such names as Jack-in-the-Green, Green George, and the Green Man. He walked in a procession through the villages, symbolizing his return as spring moves towards summer. Typically, a pretty young woman, bearing the title "Queen of the May," led the procession. She was accompanied by a young man selected as the "May King," typically symbolized by Jack-in-the-Green. The woman and man were also known as the "May Bride" and "Bridegroom," bearing flowers and other symbols of fertility related to agriculture.

An old Cornish May custom was to decorate doors and porches with green boughs of sycamore and hawthorn. In Ireland, it was once the custom to fasten a green bough against the home on the first of May to ensure an abundance of milk in the coming summer. The ancient Druids are said to have herded cattle through an open fire on this day, believing that such an act would keep the cattle from disease all year.

The connection of the tree to May celebrations is quite ancient and rooted in archaic tree worship throughout Europe. The belief that the gods dwelled within trees was widespread. Later, this tenet diminished to a belief that the spirit of vegetation resided in certain types of trees, such as the oak, ash, and hawthorn. In many parts of Europe, young people would carry branches back to their villages gathered on a May morning, suspending them in the village square from a tall pole. Bringing newly budding branches into the village was believed to renew life for everyone. Dances were performed around this "maypole" to ensure that everyone was connected or woven into the renewing forces of Nature.

The maypole is traditionally a tall pole garlanded with greenery or flowers and often hung with ribbons that are woven into complex patterns by a group of dances. Such performances are survivals of ancient dances around a living tree as part of spring rites designed to ensure fertility. Tradition varies as to the type of wood used for the maypole. In some accounts, the traditional wood is ash or birch, and in others, it is the cypress or the elm. The maypole is traceable to the *herms* (or *hermai*) that was placed at the crossroads throughout the Roman Empire.

As mentioned previously, the herms is a pillar-like figure sporting the upper torso of a god or spirit. It is a symbol of fertility and often included an erect penis protruding from the pillar. The earliest herms was simply wooden columns upon which a ritual mask was hung. In time, to reduce replacement costs, the Romans began making the herms from stone instead of wood. In May, the herms was adorned with flowers and greenery, and sacred offerings were placed before it. This and other elements of ancient Italian Paganism were carried by the Romans throughout most of continental Europe and into the British Isles.[23]

The garland of flowers, associated with May rituals, is a symbol of the inner connections between all things. The garland is a symbol of that which binds and connects. Garlands are typically made from plants and flowers that symbolize the season or event for which the garland is hung as a marker or indicator. In ancient Greek and Roman art, many goddesses carry garlands, particularly the flower goddess Flora associated with May. The maypole is often decorated with a garland as a symbol of fertility in anticipation of the coming summer and harvest season.

Among the Celtic people, the celebration of May was called Beltane. This festival celebrated the return of life and fertility to

---

23 Carl Kerenyi, *Dionysos: Archetypal Image of Indestructible Life* (Princeton University Press, 1976) 380–381.

a world that has passed through the winter season. It is the third of the four great Celtic fire festivals of the year: Beltane, Imbolc, Lughnasahd, and Samhain. Beltane was traditionally celebrated at the end of April. In modern Witchcraft, many celebrate Beltane on May 1st or May Eve. Along with its counterpart Samhain, Beltane divided the Celtic year into its two primary seasons: winter and summer. Beltane marked the beginning of summer's half and the pastoral growing season.

The word *Beltane* literally means "bright fire" and refers to the bonfires lit during this season. It may or may not be derived from the worship of the Celtic deity known as Belenus.[24] In ancient times, Beltane heralded the coming of summer and the promise of fullness. Herds of cattle were ritually driven between bonfires as an act of purification and protection. This was believed to ensure their safety and fertility throughout the remainder of the year. The fires celebrated the warmth of the Sun and its power to return life and fruitfulness to the soil.

Some Witches believe that Beltane was held in honor of the god Bel. In some modern traditions, he is also known as Beli, Balar, Balor, or Belenus. Janet and Stewart Farrar point out that some people have suggested that Bel is the Brythonic Celtic equivalent of the god Cernunnos.[25]

In some modern Witchcraft traditions, Beltane marks the appearance of the Horned One, who is the reborn solar God slain during the Wheel of the Year. He then becomes consort to the

---

24 James MacKillop, *Dictionary of Celtic Mythology* (Oxford University Press, 1998) 35.

25 Janet and Stewart Farrar, *Eight Sabbats for Witches* (Robert Hale, 1981) 80–81.

Goddess, impregnating her with his seed, and thereby ensuring his own rebirth once again.

In the evolution of god images, he became the Harvest Lord of agrarian society and is associated with the Green Man, a popular image connecting the God to the ever-returning cycle of foliage and flowering.

Honoring Ancestral Spirits

In this current age of self-development and self-focus, we can sometimes lose sight of the valuable teachings left to us by our ancestors. In Witchcraft, there is a phrase known as "the well-worn path," which refers to the knowledge left behind by those who came before us. They have blazed the trail for us, and we follow the path to its end, and then blaze our own trail into the future. It is here on the well-worn path that the New Ways meet and cross with the Old Ways.

The Old Ways of our ancestors are intimately linked to our ancestors themselves. We bear within us this ancient connection, in part because our DNA is derived from those who came before us. As occultists, Witches, and Pagans, we understand that, in a metaphysical sense, everything is linked together, one thing influencing another in an endless cycle. In a magickal sense, time is non-linear, and so the past, present, and future all flow into each other. In occult philosophy, there is no true separation. Dion Fortune, a famous occultist, taught that one could be reincarnated in the past as well as the future, and that all time periods exist simultaneously.

Remembering and honoring one's ancestors is an act of connection to one's roots. It is a bridge extending into the past across which may flow the collective consciousness of one's ancestors.

Through a formal link with the ancestral spirit, one can draw power and vigor; for it is in knowing where we came from that we come to understand who we are today. Understanding who we are prepares us to reap the harvest of what we can become tomorrow.

The ancient Etruscans worshipped their ancestors through an image known as a lasa spirit. The ancient Romans called such spirits Lare and perceived them as household spirits, guardians of home and family. Small shrines were set by the hearth or upon the mantle in remembrance of departed loved ones. On the base of the shrine was depicted a serpent, symbolizing the Underworld current connecting the living and the dead. Candles were lit before the shrine when a family member was born, wed, gave birth, or died. In this way, the ancestral spirits participated in the family event, and the momentum of the ancestral current was kept flowing within the family.

Offerings were also placed at the shrine when a new venture was undertaken, or a dilemma faced the household. The family spirits in the otherworld were believed to have power to influence the world of the living. Among the Etruscans, the primary offering" was a handful of fava beans and some wine. The Romans gave offerings of spelt grain, along with a bowl containing equal amounts of wine, milk, and honey.

By lighting a candle at the ancestral shrine and reading out loud the myths or legends associated with one's heritage, a personal alignment to the Old Ways can be established. The spoken voice creates vibrations that brings the passion of one's blood up into the ether. This creates a ripple within the Astral Plane, connecting one with times long forgotten. To strengthen this connection, one can place symbols or icons associated with one's

Honoring Ancestral Spirits

nationality in or around the shrine. It is also useful to take on a personal name that may have been used in ancient times among one's ancestors. This helps to further connect with the energies of antiquity. Reading books and viewing movies that reflect cultural heroes is also an excellent aid to alignment. These tales often transmit the link to the collective conscious of the ancient peoples who created them. Therefore, by incorporating them into one's own consciousness, one can become a part of the spiritual heritage of one's ancestors.

Preparation of an Ancestral Shrine

Select a suitable shrine structure to reflect the ancestral memory. In effect, this will be the home of your house spirit, so make it attractive and inviting. Place it upon a wall or on a mantle. Align the shrine within your home to the West or East to connect it symbolically to the rising and setting of the Sun and Moon. In this way, you create a connection to the cycles of life, death, and rebirth. Set an image in the shrine to represent the indwelling spirit.

Place a small offering bowl or vase in front of the shrine. Offerings of grain, milk, or flowers are good options. To activate the shrine, light some incense of either pine, sandalwood, or a similar earthy scent. Pass the smoke beneath the shrine so that the smoke rises through and around the shrine. While doing this, say:

> *"Spirits of the ether, awaken, gather the ancient ones here, who were of old known to my Clan. I bless this shrine in the names of (give your deity names). As it was in the time of the beginning, so is it now, so shall it be."*

At this point, the shrine has been blessed and consecrated. Sit quietly before the shrine and visualize a small, soft blue light around the figurine or statue in your shrine. In time, you will actually see this light come and go within the shrine. This is assuming that you provide an offering at each Full Moon and all family occasions such as birthdays, marriages, and so forth. Light a candle each time you sit before the shrine. Request assistance in personal matters and work towards establishing a good rapport with your household spirit.

The Witches' Circle

Although many commentators believe that the use of a ritual circle by Witches is a modern Gardnerian concept, there are much older references. As early as the seventeenth century, we find woodcut illustrations depicting Witches gathered in a ritual/magickal circle. One such example, drawn by the Italian demonologist Guazzo in 1608, appears in his book *Compendium Maleficarum*. Here, Guazzo depicts several Witches gathered in a circle traced upon the ground. Outside of the circle appears a horned figure, possibly evoked to appear by the Witches. It is interesting to note that Guazzo also mentions that Witches work with Elemental spirits of Earth, Air, Fire, and Water. In occult lore, the Elementals are known as gnomes, sylphs, salamanders, and undines.

The Witches' circle, or Circle of the Arts, is in effect a microcosm of the Witches' magickal universe. The magickal circle is traced upon the ground, traditionally nine to eighteen feet in diameter. Properly cast, it becomes a place between the physical and spiritual world. Witches often refer to the circle as the world between the worlds and as a sacred space.

Witches gathered in a circle marked upon the ground. Italian woodcut by Francesco Guazzo, from the Compendium Maleficarum, published in 1608

Once established, the circle serves to contain the magickal and metaphysical energies raised within its sphere, condensing them enough to accomplish the desired magickal effect. The threshold of the circle, through which the celebrants enter and exit, is located at various points pertaining to the inner symbolism contained in each tradition. Many traditions use the North or the East quarter. In the ancient Mystery Traditions, the Northeast point of the circle served as the doorway.

The North is the realm of the power of the gods, and the East is the realm of enlightenment. To enter and exit at the Northeast point was to symbolically meet with the gods in power and enlightenment. When a circle is established according to the mystical associations unique to each tradition, it becomes a grotto for initiation and spiritual rebirth, the sacred womb of the Mother Goddess.

The circle is first marked out physically so that a vehicle exists wherein the Elemental spirits can be invoked. A space is marked out to separate the mundane from the sacred. The Elements are then evoked at each of the four quarters of the circle according to their correspondence. Traditionally, the Element of Earth is assigned to the North. Elemental Air is placed at the East, Fire at the South, and Water at the West. Depending upon the climate conditions of the region in which any tradition abides, these Elemental associations may vary.

The ritual or magickal circle should be visualized as a sphere of energy rather than a wall of energy enclosing the area. The sphere serves to seal not only the circumference, but also the top and bottom of the sacred space that one has established. Traditionally, beings known as the Watchers are evoked to each of the four quarters of the circle to magickally guard the sacred area against the intrusion of any forces not in harmony with the ritual. The Watchers also bear witness to the rites and can exert a great deal of influence over the nature of the work at hand.

Movement within the ritual circle is always performed in a clockwise manner when creating sacred space or magickal workings. When dissolving the circle or negating magickal energy, the movements are always counterclockwise (note that in the Southern Hemisphere, this is reversed). Wiccans refer to this as *deosil* (sunwise) and *widdershins* (or *tuathal*, against the shadows). According to the Mystery Teachings, the clockwise movement within the circle symbolizes the emergence of lunar or feminine energies from the left side, displacing the solar or masculine energies associated with the right side. It is the Moon rising to claim the Heavens as the Sun departs to the Underworld. Since Wicca is a matrifocal and lunar sect, it is only natural to find this association. The solar associations of movement within the circle stem from the Indo-European influences that usurped the matrifocal concepts, particularly in central Europe.

Once established, the ritual circle serves to accumulate energy. The participants within the sphere are immersed in the energies being drawn to, or raised within, the sacred sphere. As an attendant within the circle, one becomes aligned with the frequency or vibrational rate of the current of energy present. In ancient times, it was held that the power of a Witch arose from an unbroken participation in the rituals of the year. Such participation aligned one with the natural flow of earth's energy. Becoming attuned with Nature freed one's psychic abilities and made available certain insights that helped one to develop magickal powers.

The Rites of Summer

The summer solstice marks the longest day of the year and is an important festival occasion in some modern Witchcraft traditions. In popular lore, the summer solstice marks the battle between the Oak King and Holly King, figures representing the waxing and waning forces of Nature. On the day of the summer solstice, the Holly King defeats his brother the Oak King. Even though this is the longest day of the year, the days begin to grow shorter from this time forward, leading then into the fall season. In these traditions, it is for this reason that the Holly King reigns at the summer solstice, for he is the lord of the waning forces of Nature.

In southern Europe, groups such as the Benandanti enacted ritual battles. Fennel and sorghum stalks were used as symbols of light and darkness in a battle over the fertility of crops and herds. A period of time (three days prior to a solstice or equinox) known as the "ember days" was fought over by the forces of light and darkness. It was believed that during this time, a doorway opened between the worlds, one that could influence the delicate balance of the seasons. For this reason, the forces of light had to be vigilant in order to ward off any contamination of the season by the waning forces. In Italian Witchcraft, the summer solstice is the celebration of the anticipation of plenty, the bounty of Nature, and the coming of the harvest season.

In some Witchcraft traditions, the summer solstice festival is called Litha. The word *litha* may well be derived from the Anglo-Saxon word *lida*, which means "Moon." Some commentators have suggested that the month *aerra lida* corresponded to the month of June in the Anglo-Saxon calendar, while *afterra lida* corresponded to July. Some Witches believe that Litha was actually the ancient name of the summer solstice, although there is no historical evidence to confirm this. In the popular fictional work titled *The Return of the King* by J.R.R. Tolkien, the author uses the word *lithe* to denote Midsummer Day. Some commentators feel this may be the origin of the word's appearance in modern Wicca. The use of the word Litha to indicate the summer solstice first publicly appears in modern Wicca in the late 1970s in such works as the Spiral Dance by Starhawk.

The summer solstice is also connected with fairy lore. On Midsummer Eve, the fairy race is said to gather in grand celebration of Nature. A ring of mushrooms, or a depressed circle of grass or brush, is often called a fairy ring. To spot one on the morning of the summer solstice was believed to be a sign that the fairies had gathered there. Great care had to be taken to ensure that the fairy ring remained undisturbed. In some traditions, Witches would cast their ritual circle near a fairy ring and celebrate the summer solstice in a place held sacred by the fairies.

Because of the many "supernatural" elements associated with summer, various techniques of divination were believed to be particularly potent. In rural villages, people would break open hens' eggs on Midsummer Eve and look for omens within the contents. The placing of the yarrow beneath the pillow on Midsummer Eve was

The Rites of Summer

thought to reveal one's future mate in a dream. Mugwort picked on the summer solstice and passed through the flames of a bonfire was believed to create a talisman of protection.

One of the most powerful herbs associated with the summer solstice was St. John's wort. In folk magick, this herb was sometimes called "demon's flight" due to its reputation for dispelling evil. In Italian Witchcraft, attaching St. John's wort to a stalk of fennel can protect entryways from negative spirits that attempt to gain access to the home. Special liqueur is also made from raw walnuts picked on the summer solstice. This liqueur is called *nocino* and is consumed the following summer solstice. The power assigned to plants on this day is linked to the power of light at the summer solstice, the longest day of the year.

In this type of magickal reasoning, the plants would retain the power of the waxing forces of Nature if picked on this day. Such plants could then be used to deal with the spirits of the waning forces of Nature.

The Mystery Tradition Within Wicca

A Mystery Tradition contains a set of concepts taught to initiates that imparts an understanding of its inner mechanisms, which in turn empowers the theology of the religion or spiritual tradition. Within Wicca, we find the basic Mystery Teachings of pre-Christian Europe. Mystery Teachings evolved side-by-side with the evolution of the human brain and its ability to analyze and conceptualize. Added to this was experimentation, accidental or otherwise, concerning altered states of consciousness.

It was the village shaman who experimented with various plant substances that allowed them to more fully descend into altered states of consciousness. In many of the themes reflected in the Mystery Tradition, time is not linear, but cyclical. It has no beginning, no middle point, and no end. This becomes obvious in the classical myths of goddesses who give birth to their lovers or brothers and are then impregnated by them so they can be born of her. Only lunar myths reflect this non-linear concept of time, which is why the Moon is the symbol of the Mysteries.

The word "mystery" is derived from the Greek verb *myein*, meaning "to close," and refers to closing one's lips as in remaining silent or to closing one's eyes and seeing within. The blindfold used in many Wiccan-inspired initiation ceremonies is a symbol of entering into the Mysteries. The removal of the blindfold opens the eyes of the initiate to behold the sacred tools and symbols of Wicca, highlighted by the flickering candles and accented by the magickal fragrance of burning incense. This action imprints upon the initiate's psyche and serves to activate the dormant psychic nature sleeping within the subconscious mind.

It is in the Mystery Tradition that an individual comes to discover their own role within a Wiccan-based spiritual path. As mentioned earlier, the experiences and teachings of those who have gone before encompass the well-worn path. Where the path ends is the threshold through which the individual must pass on their own. This is the quest that one must make to obtain enlightenment and gain liberation from the Cycle of Rebirth. Once the teachings of those who have gone before are assimilated, the Witch can then extend the well-worn path for others to follow later. This is the intuitive practice of Wiccan-inspired Witchcraft, where the practitioner can leave their own unique footprints along the extended path. Joseph Campbell summed it up nicely with the following:

"Furthermore, we have not even to risk the adventure alone; for the heroes of all time have gone before us; the labyrinth is thoroughly known; we have only to follow the thread of the hero-path. And where we had thought to find an abomination, we shall find a god; where we had thought to slay another, we shall slay ourselves; where we had thought to travel outward, we shall come to the center of our own existence; where we had thought to be alone, we shall be with all the world." [26]

---

[26] Joseph Campbell, *The Hero with a Thousand Faces* (New World Library, 2008) 18.

Essentially, a Mystery Tradition contains two main focuses. First is the understanding of the inner mechanism within Nature. To this category belongs such knowledge as the inner teachings of magick, rituals, spell casting, divination, and so forth. Second is the understanding of the soul and its relationship to Divinity and the Universe. In this category, we would place things like personal power, the Cycle of Rebirth, personal enlightenment, the gods, astral dimensions, the Threefold Law, the journey of the soul, the Summerland, and so forth.

The essential mythos of the Mystery Tradition contained within Wiccan-inspired traditions is centered upon the Wheel of the Year. This is the foundation of the belief in ever-returning cycles, an aspect of which encompasses the belief in reincarnation. Death and the survival of the soul or spirit are important elements of the Mystery Teachings. Wicca is essentially an agrarian Mystery Tradition wherein the aspects of plowing, planting, growing, and harvesting are all symbolic depictions of the journey of the soul.

The Agricultural Mysteries are involved with loss, return, death, and rebirth. This is best depicted in the myth of Demeter and Persephone. They are also involved with the transformations associated with changes in states of mythos of consciousness. This incorporates the use of psychotropic plants such as hallucinogenic mushrooms or various fermented liquids. We refer to this aspect as the Fermentation Mysteries. These Teachings also include the Harvest Mysteries, which symbolically reveal the Mysteries through various myths of dying gods.

The Slain God or Divine King is an integral part of Wiccan-inspired Mysteries. He is intimately connected to the life cycle of the plant kingdom and shares the attributes associated with planting and harvesting. His blood contains the same vital life-giving principle as does the seed and therefore must return into the soil for there to be life and abundance in the coming year. The Slain God mythos retains the earlier lunar mysteries of the Great Goddess cult. The Divine King reflects the solar mysteries of the Indo-European cults. In Wicca, these have blended together into one mythos.

In the Wiccan mythos, the seasonal cycles of Nature comprise what is known as the waxing and waning tides of the Earth. These are the forces of growth and decline, the old making way for the new. There are two sets of mythical figures (depending upon the tradition) that represent these tides. The first is the Oak King and the Holly King, common in popular lore. The second is the Stag and the Wolf, found in many Traditions of southern Europe. Their myths are tales of life and death, one succeeding the other in an ever-repeating cycle.

The Mystery Tradition associated with fermentation is an essential element of the Transformation Mysteries. The Teachings of the Grain are intimately connected to the Fermentation Mysteries and are probably best reflected in the Eleusinian Mysteries. The dry seed being planted in the soil is symbolic of death, the descent into the Underworld.

The mystical meeting beneath the soil with the inherent properties of decay eventually results in the awakening of new life within the seed. This is the meeting of the Goddess with the Lord of the Underworld. The emergence of physical life from the seed, pushing up towards the surface, is symbolic of the process of rebirth within the Underworld. It is the beginning of the ascent of the Goddess and her return to the world of the living.

The Mystery Tradition Within Wicca

The appearance of the young sprout, having broken through the soil, is symbolic of rebirth into the physical dimension, the return of the Goddess. However, the plant itself is the God, the Child of Promise. The spiritual and mystical process described here is itself the Goddess. She is the spirit, and he is the body. Thus, in time, this newborn god will become the Harvest Lord. His life energy will be returned to the earth where it will impregnate the Goddess. His seed will be sown in her womb and new life will issue forth once again.

The essence of the God is contained in the seed or grain, or in the grape (the blood as is the case concerning Dionysus). The intoxicating power of fermented grain was believed to be the presence of the God within one's body. This ancient concept is the basis for the Wiccan rite of cakes and wine and the Christian rite of communion. To consume the God was to take on his nature. To take on the nature of the God was to align oneself with him and thus inherit his power of resurrection. Through union with the God, death lost its power and rebirth was assured.

In the ancient Mystery Teachings of the Mediterranean region, which includes Egypt, Greece, and Rome, to free the initiate from the fear of death was essential to the functioning of the sect. This is why great care was taken with techniques to ensure the soul existed beyond the life of the body. Such rites were performed in the pyramids of Egypt and in underground chambers in both Greece and Rome. Here, the initiate experienced a form of astral projection and came away with the realization that the body was merely a temporary vessel for a timeless spirit.

Exploring the Legend of the Descent of the Goddess

In modern Wicca, the Myth of the *Descent of the Goddess* is still one of the primary texts of Wiccan theology. Even in some Celtic-inspired traditions, this mythos is employed, even though it does not appear in Celtic mythology. The essence of the myth is traceable to the ancient cultures of the Tigris-Euphrates region.

Its classical form appears in Greek mythology and was the cornerstone of the Eleusinian Mystery Cult. The *Legend of the Descent* is, on the exoteric level, a story about the Goddess entering the Underworld and meeting the Lord of the Underworld. On the esoteric level, the tale is one of the journeys of our own souls as they enter the physical dimension. For we are not physical beings having a spiritual experience; instead, we are spiritual beings having a human experience.

The popular version of the *Legend of the Descent* depicts the Goddess departing into the Underworld. The Goddess seeks the Harvest Lord, her lover who was sacrificed in the fields. In the Mystery Tradition, she is joined in sexual union with the Lord of the Underworld and is impregnated with the Child of Promise. The Child of Promise is the newborn sun god who is given birth on the winter solstice. On the spring equinox, the Goddess returns again to the earth from the Underworld.

The esoteric version of the *Legend of the Descent* differs from the popular version, but contains the same theme. The mythos behind the Legend is built upon the concept that the Goddess was originally incomplete or imbalanced in the integration of her totality.

To possess the knowledge of all things, or to assimilate her opposite polarity, she descended into the Underworld and experienced decline and physical death. Her journey to the Underworld is symbolic of her passage through the currents flowing between the worlds; and so, she journeyed to the Underworld in her boat, upon the Sacred River of Descent.

As the myth unfolds, the Goddess is stopped at a series of seven gates. At each gate, she encounters the demand for payment by the guardians of the gate. The seven gates are symbolic of the seven planes or dimensions of manifestation within occult cosmology. According to the tale, the Goddess surrenders an article of clothing as payment for passage. This symbolizes the casting off of self-identity. A surrendering of the self in order to obtain enlightenment is an ancient theme found not only in the Mystery Tradition, but also in such public religions as Christianity and Buddhism.

At the first gate, the Goddess relinquishes her scepter, which is a symbol of her personal power and her ability to extend influence outwardly over other things and situations. The loss of personal power or recognition isolates her and brings the focus of the Universe directly upon her own existence. The second gate requires her crown, symbolic of her authority. Here, she loses the outward symbol of her power. With her personal power relinquished, so too dissolves her symbols.

Exploring the Legend of the Descent of the Goddess

The guardian of the third gate requires her necklace. This item is symbolic of her claim to personal value, her achievements, and accomplishments. Wealth is often viewed as a sign of personal power, as it states that the individual is successful and influential according to the standards of the society in which the person operates. At the fourth gate, the Goddess removes her ring. The ring is symbolic of class level and personal labelling. The ring denotes relationships and signifies membership in organizations, orders, lodges, and various religious systems. To remove the ring is to stand alone without connection, association, or definition.

The guardian of the fifth gate requires the Goddess to relinquish her girdle. In ancient cultures, the girdle symbolized social status. On the subconscious level, it is the symbol of the personal facade. To relinquish the girdle is to open the self to examination. In ancient Rome, the girdle was worn by a woman as an outward symbol that she had reached maturity. When the woman was to marry, her parents would tie a knot upon the girdle, which was later untied by her husband on their wedding night. A married woman continued to wear the girdle, which her husband had knotted again after the wedding night. The knot was untied once more when the woman gave birth to her first-born child, and then her girdle was dedicated to Artemis and no longer worn. In ancient times, the meaning of a virgin was a woman who had not yet given birth, and so she lost her virginity during labor. Therefore, the girdle could no longer be worn in public.

At the sixth gate, the Goddess removes her sandals. In the ancient Cult of Hecate, an Underworld goddess among other aspects, the sandal was a symbol of the power to enter and exit from the Underworld at will. High level initiates of Hecate wore bronze sandals as a sign of their status and of their power. To surrender her sandals was to surrender her power to leave at will and therefore experience the descent fully in all its elements.

At the seventh and last gate, the Goddess drops her gown as the final payment to the Guardians of the Portals. The gown is the covering of the fragile veneer of self. The self isolates the spirit from the whole of spiritual experience. Once the gown is removed, the spirit may join in union with the community of spirits. This is reflected in the Wiccan practice of celebrating in the nude (known as skyclad).

At this point in the myth, the Goddess is brought to the Lord of the Underworld. She stands naked before him, and he is so struck with her beauty that he kneels before her. This is the meeting of life and death, increase and decline. The Lord of the Underworld tempts her to remain with him and to embrace his realm of existence. This is the temptation to end all strife, but it calls for a union with her opposite upon his terms. This is not a state of balance, and the Goddess recognizes it.

Accordingly, the Goddess resists the Lord of the Underworld and protests his role in the decline of life. Since she will not embrace him freely, he compels her to accept his scourge. He teaches her that he is not responsible for decline and death; his role is as comforter and transformer of those who have crossed over. Thus, the Goddess passes into an understanding of her opposite polarity and incorporates it in her own consciousness. This is reflected in her proclamation of newfound love for the Dark Lord.

Next, the legend reveals that the Lord and Lady unveil their respective mysteries to each other. The Goddess receives the necklace of rebirth, which is symbolic of the connective link between the worlds, the inner mechanism. The Dark Lord receives the cauldron of rebirth, which is symbolic of manifested power. In the myth, we are told that they love one another and become one. Here, we find the obtainment of balance between life and death. No longer are they enemies, but equal participants in a cycle of renewal. The three mysteries in the life of humankind are revealed: birth, life, and death. Sex becomes the gateway to life from the Underworld, birth is the renewal, and death is the transformation whereby old age becomes youth again. Just as a person must sleep for their body to be refreshed, so too must the soul rest and renew itself in the sleep of the Underworld.

The legend continues with the Mystery Teaching concerning reincarnation. Here, we are told that we must meet, recognize, remember, and love anew. The final passages in the legend address the issue of the enlightenment gained by the Goddess herself in the descent. Thus, to be one of her hidden children is to descend into the shadows and unite with her mythos. In doing so, the soul aligns with her renewal and unites with her spiritually (the way of her communion). In ancient reasoning, the Sun (and Moon) descended into the Underworld at night, returning home. For light was at home in the darkness, which is one of the Mystery Teachings. This is one of the reasons why all goddesses of the Underworld are depicted in art carrying torches. They bear the light within the darkness.

In the last verses, we find that the magick, whereby we become aligned to the Goddess, resides between the worlds. The magick circle on this plane is the ritual circle wherein we celebrate the Wheel of the Year and the lunar rites.

Once properly cast, the circle moves between the worlds, and we are magickally aligned with the Goddess. As above, so below. The circle upon the planes is the unfolding of the *Legend of the Descent* whereby we encounter the Dark Lord and inherit the legacy passed to her in this Realm of Shadows: the legacy of renewal and rebirth.

The Tarot Magician: An Occult Tradition

There is a certain degree of debate today over whether the Magician of the Tarot as we now know him is the same figure as depicted in early Tarot decks. In the Tarot, the traditional placement of the Magician follows the Fool card. Two of the earliest images of the Magician appearing numerically within the Major Arcana depict either a cobbler (shoemaker), a juggler, or a curious figure sitting at a table with a variety of objects spread out before him. This latter figure is often referred to as the slight-of-hand artist or the swindler. The most common image of this is the shell game where a pea is hidden under one of three walnut shells, which are quickly mixed while the performer talks to distract the onlooker.

Some modern commentators feel that these early characters were not of an occult nature and represent a different figure from the Magician altogether. In exploring the origins of the Magician card, we will examine the early character of the cobbler or shoemaker and look at the other characters as well. The word "cobbler" comes from the Middle English word *cobeler*. The archaic meaning of the word is a bungler or "one who is clumsy." This seems at first glance to be an odd association with the shoemaker. The word "clumsy" is derived from the Scandinavian *clomsen* and the Icelandic *klunni*. Interestingly, these are the root words of the clown, buffoon, and jester as well. The word "jester" is ultimately derived from the Latin *gestusus*, which means "to gesticulate." Gesticulation is to make gestures, especially while speaking. This is the art employed by the slight-of-hand expert.

But why was the cobbler associated with the concept of being clumsy? The answer may lie in an ancient magickal tradition that features the sandal. From the ancient writings of Empedocles and from those written about him, the Cult of Hecate is frequently mentioned. Here, we find the bronze sandal as a symbol of the magician of Hecate, possibly linked to silver sandals appearing in sixth-century Babylonian practices associated with the god Adad and his wife Shala.

In *Ancient Philosophy, Mystery, and Magic* by Peter Kingsley, we read: *"The bronze sandal [...] was the magical 'symbol' par excellence of Hecate. Worn or held by the magician, it was the 'sign' of his ability to descend to the underworld at will."* [27]

Legends surrounding Empedocles as an initiate of the Cult of Hecate insist that he wore a bronze sandal. To move about in a bronze sandal would indeed at the very least give the appearance of being clumsy, if not define clumsiness itself. It is interesting to

---

27 Peter Kingsley, *Ancient Philosophy, Mystery, and Magic* (Oxford University Press, 1995) 245.

note that, in Norse lore, we find a legendary blacksmith known as Wayland the Smith. He was incapacitated by command of King Nidud of Sweden so that he could not escape, and he was compelled into his service. In his earlier tales, Wayland is actually king of the gnomes and produced metal amulets and magickal swords. The association of gnomes with earthen caverns and the association of Hecate's magician with the underworld are equally noteworthy in our discussion.

On a side note, it is curious that the Latin and Scandinavian words for clumsy are both from cultures in which we find figures whose feet are encumbered due to their office, who make shoes, and who are connected to metal in a magickal way.

By the end of the sixth century BCE, we find writings by Heraclitus of Ephesus that attack magicians as swindlers and tricksters who use deception to persuade people into believing they have magickal power. Despite this, magick continued to thrive over the centuries, and magicians were viewed as theurgists. A theurgist is one who performs divine actions chiefly with the aid of magickal symbols. This is the image of the Neoplatonic magician, who possessed the ability to make rain, stop plagues, and to both extract and replace the soul of an individual at will. According to Kingsley, Neoplatonic theurgists also had *"visionary encounters"* with Hecate.[28]

Now that we have seen evidence of an occult tradition associated with the shoe, what of the slight-of-hand artist? One of the earliest images of this Tarot figure depicts a table set with a cup and several round balls. Commentators are unsure what the balls are, but most suggest something akin to bread. It is quite likely that these balls are the type used in aleuromancy. Aleuromancy is a form of divination in which various outcomes or situations are written on small strips

---

28   Ibid.

of paper. This form of divination was popular in the temples of Apollo who, as patron of this art, was known as Aleuromantis. In aleuromancy, each strip is then folded and rolled up into a small ball of dough (very much like a fortune cookie). Each ball of dough is then covered with a walnut shell. Walnuts were believed to have oracular properties by the Greeks and Romans. The shells are mixed nine times, and then people pick a shell, retrieving the strip of paper to learn of their fortune. Here, we see a possible connection of the early Tarot image of the slight-of-hand artist with an oracle of the god Apollo, an association with divination. Divination itself has long been the providence of underworld deities, which brings us back to Hecate and the magician or priest.

One of the sacred cult objects of Hecate was a triangular plaque with a rod rising from the center. Mounted on the rod was a flat disk. This tool was the standard design in ancient times for the working surface of the cobbler. On the disk, leather was placed; the rod allowed height so that sandal straps could hang down and be laced around the disk to the other side of the sandal. Since the sandal was the sign of the magician's ability to descend into the underworld at will, it may be that the polished disk also doubled as a type of scrying mirror for divination.

Professor Kingsley depicts the tradition of Empedocles and the Neoplatonist theurgists as heirs of the mystical sect of Hecate and the associations discussed in this article. With the renewed interest in Hermetics during the Renaissance in Italy, it is likely that the theurgist recognized the symbolism of the cobbler in Tarot, the secret revealed only in symbol and not in name. Within a short period, the Tarot symbolism would change to rightly reflect the cobbler and the slight-of-hand artist as representative of the theurgist and magician.

The Full Moon in Witchcraft Rituals

"Whenever ye have need of anything, once in the month and when the Moon is full, ye shall assemble in some secret place, or in a forest all together join to adore the potent spirit of your queen, my mother, great Diana. She who fain would learn all sorcery yet has not won its deepest secrets, them my mother will teach her, in truth all things as yet unknown. And ye shall be freed from slavery, and so ye shall be free in everything; and as a sign that ye are truly free, ye shall be naked in your rites, both men and women also..."

- Charles Leland, *Aradia: Gospel of the Witches (1899)*

The Goddess of the Moon was traditionally worshipped in groves by a lake or spring. She was also worshipped in a grotto where water issued forth from between the rocks. Her priestesses were required to take special care of the water. A sacred fire in the grove or grotto represented the light of the Moon, and a strict custom existed that it must be kept from being extinguished. This was rooted in the belief that the Moon Goddess was the light of the fire itself, and, in ancient times, it was believed that fire could lie latent in wood. In early times, the security of the divine fire required an ample supply of sacred wood that was dried and readily available in her grove or grotto. Later in history, lamps replaced the use of wood. The liquid symbolism was still intact, as the lamp fuel was often olive oil, which again connected the fire back to the wood of the olive tree. There is an interesting legend in which the goddess Diana is smuggled out of Greece inside a bundle of branches and delivered to Lake Nemi in Italy. Thus, Diana was the latent flame within the wood, awaiting rebirth in her new grove. The bundle of branches in which she arrived was the first supply of her torches.

In the grove of the Moon Goddess, torches lighted the sacred woods. The festival of Diana, celebrated on August 13th, was always marked by a multitude of torches that reflected their light off the water of Lake Nemi and filled her sacred grove with a holy aura. The Moon Goddess herself belonged to the torch-bearing class of deities who themselves were always connected in some manner with the Underworld. The Underworld connection linked the Moon Goddess to the Fates, so the power of divination was bestowed upon her worshippers.

The image of Witches gathered beneath the Full Moon is well imprinted on the human psyche. Ritual and magickal practices have been associated with Witchcraft since ancient times. Greek and Roman writings tell us that Witches had the ability to call or draw the Moon down from the night sky.

The Greek writer Aristophanes in his work titled *Clouds* mentions using a Witch to draw down the Moon into a box "like they do mirrors." (It is interesting to note that beech wood was widely used for making boxes in the Aegean or Mediterranean region, and that beech wood was also associated with Witchcraft.) The mention of mirrors refers to an ancient practice that involved

The Full Moon in Witchcraft Rituals

reflecting the Full Moon in a jar or dish filled to the brim with water and using the water as an ingredient in various preparations.

In the old rites, the ritual circle was formed near a running stream and before a tree that is not gnarled or misshapen. This is because, in archaic Pagan belief, evil spirits cannot cross running water and generally fear it. This ensured the safety of all within the ritual circle, for to open the portals to the otherworld allowed both good and evil spirits to enter the world of humankind. The tree served also as a guardian that stood between the worlds. In ancient lore, trees were believed to possess the power to bind spirits either inside the trunks or entangled within the roots.

The circle itself symbolized the Full Moon above. In Italian Witchcraft, the art of mimicry is employed to attract that which is desired. Therefore, the resemblance of the circle to the shape of the Moon created a link. The ritual circle was drawn on the ground with a beech wood wand. Theophrastus mentions the beech tree as one of the most common trees in the Apennines and the lowlands of Latium. Beech wood was used to form the first pages of books (as opposed to scrolls) and became associated with preserving ancient wisdom. The beech tree is also associated with serpents, as noted by Tennyson, who refers to the "serpent-rooted" beech. In this lies the connection of the wand as a tool of ancestral invocation. The serpent, in ancient Italic Paganism, was symbolic of the ancestral line within the Underworld. Ancestral shrines in Roman homes bore a portrait of the head of the household flanked by two Lares spirits, and below these figures appears a snake stretched horizontally across the bottom of the shrine.

The significance of the beech wand and the ritual circle take on greater meaning when we explore ancient beliefs concerning the Moon. In the Aegean region, souls of the dead were believed to abide on the Moon. As the Moon received these souls, the Moon increased in fullness. Therefore, the Full Moon symbolized the gathering of our ancestors. And, just as they assembled above, so too did the kindred below fill the ritual circle. The ancient Roman writer Horace, along with others of his period, wrote that Witches used a book containing chants that could call the Moon down from the sky. Here, beneath the Full Moon, the world of the living and the dead were joined together.

An archaic belief in ancient Italy held that the spirits of the dead gathered and dwelled in the air. They were said to wrap themselves in this element and thereby become invisible. One aspect of the old Full Moon rituals involved inviting the spirits of the dead to join in the celebration of the ritual circle. They were invoked overhead above the circle and a leaping dance began in which the living celebrants jumped up, dancing in the wind with their ancestors. Variations of this included dancing with an upturned broom, held aloft, that served to symbolize the ancestral spirit.

Over time, a version of this ritual dance migrated into folk-dance tradition. One related dance is known as "La Volta." The folk dance first appears in literary references from Provence, Italy as a peasant dance in the early sixteenth century. It was introduced later into Switzerland, then to France (Volte), and finally in Germany. The name *volta* means "turning." It is said that the Italian Volta was first introduced by the Count of Sault to the Paris Court in 1556.

Later, around 1581, Catherine De Medici introduced the Volta to the French court of Versailles. The Volta is said to be the first of the waltzes, or the forerunner of the waltz when combined with other round dances. A type of dance movement called the "Tordion" was used for a few measures to start the Volta.

During the Volta, the man faces his partner instead of standing alongside or opposite each other (which was considered very scandalous during this era) and holds her very close. The leader turns his partner around several times and then helps her take a high leap into the air (with the skirts shamelessly flying up). He, at times, leaps with her.

The Volta was usually taken with two single steps and a double step, and was done in three-quarter time. The dancers, with their right foot raised high in the air, hopped on the left and turned at a ninety-degree angle. They then took a long stride, another quarter turn, and then sprang high in the air, again making another quarter turn. Each pattern consisted of three-quarter turns and a leap. This peasant dance was proclaimed shameful and indecent by the upper class, who considered the entire dance to be nasty and lewd.

The records of the Inquisition at Como mention the Volta dance. It was described as having such incredible steps that it left onlookers in awe. At Como and Brescia, children between eight and twelve years old, who had once attended sabbats before being reclaimed by the Inquisition, performed this dance for the Inquisitors. The learned men of the period concluded that, because the dance was so difficult and skillful, it could only have been learned directly from the devil.

Thoughts of lewd conduct lie at the essence of the fertility nature of the Full Moon dance, which increased the possibility of returning the departed spirits to life among their own kind once again. This brings us to one of the chief reasons (all of which are related to the Moon's light) why Witches originally gathered beneath the Full Moon.

After tracing a circle on the ground to symbolize the Full Moon, Witches gathered within it and drew down her light in ritual ecstasy. Chanting, drumming, dancing, and merriment of all kinds created altered states of consciousness. Just as ancient belief held that the flame could be awakened from a log, so too could the inner light of worshipers be awakened by the Full Moon.

Gathering beneath the light of the Full Moon served to allow the Moon's light to impart fertility. The Witches would remove their clothing so as not to obstruct the light. The fertility they desired was not only of the body, but it was also of the mind and spirit. This is reflected in the closing ritual prayer of a Full Moon ceremony:

"...When our bodies lie resting nightly, speak to our inner spirits, teach us all Your Holy Mysteries. I believe Your ancient promise that we who seek Your Holy Presence will receive of Your wisdom. Behold, O' Ancient Goddess, we have gathered beneath the Full Moon at this appointed time. Now the Full Moon shines upon us. Hear us. Recall Your ancient promise..."

Various aspects of Neolithic religion lie at the foundation of lunar ritual, many of which are related to Moon worship and matrifocal imagery. It was during the Neolithic period that the foundation for the divine and magickal nature of the Moon itself was created. Images of the Moon displaying a full circle, flanked by left and right facing crescents, appear as early as 4500-4300 BCE. A coiled serpent flanked by these crescent shapes also appears during the same period. The association of two crescents flanking the full circle would seem to indicate that the ancients had a type of triformis concept about the Moon or the power of the Moon. These may be some of the earliest images suggesting a belief in the Moon as something more than a mysterious light in the sky.

Indeed, the presence of a coiled snake as a Moon symbol appears to express the idea of movement and change, a primitive attempt to explain the force that caused the Moon to change its appearance each month. This ancient connection of the serpent with the Moon continued for several thousand years, appearing in such deities as Proserpina who was worshipped by the Witches of classical Greco-Roman times. The symbols of Proserpina appear on the Witch charm known as the cimaruta.

In addition to the ability of the Moon to change shape, the ancients ascribed magickal qualities to its subtle light. Several writers of the classical era wrote that the Moon's light made plants and animals fertile. The morning dew itself was believed to be a magickal water left by moonlight, and in some folk magick books, a woman is said to be made fertile by lying nude in a meadow and rolling around in the morning dew. In the Aegean and Mediterranean region, the Moon Goddess was also known as the All-Dewy-One. The priestesses of the Moon Goddess possessed knowledge of the magickal practices that could evoke and direct the fertilizing power of the Moon. This brings us full circle back to the rural setting of the ritual circle near running water.

Working with Magick Mirrors

The magick mirror is one of the oldest tools employed in the art of both divination and spell casting. The classic magick mirror is a dark concave surface of reflective material. You can construct one for yourself by using the curved glass face of a clock and painting the convex side with glossy black paint. Antique stores are a good source for old clocks with rounded glass faces.

The traditional preparation of a magick mirror begins on the night of the Full Moon. It is particularly effective to do this when the Moon is in the sign of Pisces, Cancer, or Scorpio. Consult an astrological calendar for the days and times within any given month. Once you have painted the glass and it has thoroughly dried, bathe the mirror in an herbal brew of equal parts rosemary, fennel, rue, vervain, ivy, and walnut leaves or walnut bark. If you want to hold to the oldest of traditions, pour some sea foam into the mixture. If you are unable to obtain these items, consult a book on magickal herbs and substitute other herbs associated with psychic vision, oracles, or divination. While the glass is still bathing in the potion, hold both your hands out over it, palms down, and say:

Raven's Call

> *"I awaken the sleeping spirits of old,*
> *whose eyes reveal all that in darkness is told,*
> *give to me visions within this dark well,*
> *and make this a portal of magickal spell."*

Visualize a silver mist forming around the mirror. Take a deep breath and then slowly exhale outward upon the potion. Mentally envision that your breath moves the silver mist into the mirror. Repeat this three times. Next, remove the mirror from the potion and dry it off thoroughly. Prop the mirror up vertically with a sturdy object and make sure the support does not obscure the mirror. Hold your right hand out in front of you so that your palm is facing the convex side of the mirror. Then, place the left palm facing the concave side, about three inches away from the glass surface. You are now ready to magnetize the mirror to your aura. With the left hand, begin making a circular clockwise motion—staying within the dimensions of the mirror. Do this for a few minutes and then perform the same motion on the convex side of the mirror with the right hand. The opposite hand is always held still while the moving hand circulates. Once completed, take the mirror out beneath the Full Moon so that its light falls upon the concave side. Slowly fill the glass to the brim with the herbal potion. Hold it up towards the Moon, almost level with your eyes. Don't worry about any spillage that may take place. While looking at the Moon, allow your eyes to slightly defocus. If you are doing this correctly, you will see three rays of light emanating from the Moon. Continue to squint until the vertical line coming from the bottom of the Moon seems to touch upon the mirror. Once the moonbeam is touching the mirror, speak these words:

Working with Magick Mirrors

*"Three are the lights
here now that are seen,
but not to all
the one in-between,
for now the Enchantress
has long come at last,
to charge and empower
this dark magick glass."*

Quickly close your eyes so that you break eye contact. Open them again looking down towards the glass. Kneel and pour out the potion upon the earth as a libation. Then rinse the mirror off with fresh clear water and dry it thoroughly. The final step in preparing the mirror is to glue a strip of snakeskin to the back (convex) side. The snake is a symbol of the Underworld, which has long been associated with divination, oracle, and fate. Once the glue has dried under the snakeskin, wrap the mirror in a silk cloth to protect its lunar magnetism. Never allow sunlight to fall directly upon the mirror. The mirror is now ready to be used for divination or spell casting. Divination is the ability to see what patterns are forming towards manifestation. What you see is what is likely to occur if nothing changes the pattern being woven in the astral material.

The following technique will provide you the foundation for performing the art of divination known as scrying. Place two candles as your source of light. The light should not reflect directly upon the mirror (off a foot or two in front of you, flanking the mirror, should do it). Next, perform a series of hand passes over the mirror, slowly and deliberately.

Magickally speaking, the right hand is of an electrical nature or active charge, and the left hand is of a magnetic or receptive charge.

Raven's Call

A left-handed pass will attract an image towards formation, and right-handed passes will strengthen or focus the image. Begin by making left-handed passes over the mirror in a clockwise circle, just a few inches above it (palm open and facing down). Stop and gaze into the dark reflection, not at it, but into it. You will need to repeat these passes as you await the vision. Alternate between the left hand and the right hand. This requires patience and time. Use your intuition as you sit before the mirror. Make sure the setting is quiet and without distractions.

The magick mirror can also be used for spell casting. This simple technique involves reflections or sigils. Light two candles and set them off to each side of the mirror about three inches away. Place a photograph, image, or sigil of the target of your spell so that it reflects in the mirror. Gaze into the mirror and imagine the desired effect. Make up a short rhyme if you like so you can state your desire without breaking your concentration. If you desire to be rid of an influence or situation, you can sigilize it and then burn the sigil, gazing into the reflected flames in the mirror. Another effective method is to gently blow incense smoke onto the mirror as you gaze at the reflection. Allow yourself to stir your emotions, deeply inhale, and then slowly exhale across a stick of incense. Imagine the smoke to be a magickal vapor carrying your will. As it touches the mirror, imagine the target responding as you wish it to. Do this three times. Creating a short rhyme for your spell can be helpful in this technique as well. Once you are finished, combine the melted wax, ashes from the incense, and the photo or image you used. Dispose of this in a manner keeping with the Elemental nature of your spell. Matters of love and feelings generally belong to Water. Creative or artistic ventures belong to Air. Situations of loss, separation, or destruction can be

Working with Magick Mirrors

associated with Fire. Endurance, strength, fertility, and stability are typically linked to Earth. When disposing of ritual remnants, bear in mind that to toss something into moving water will merge it with the Water Element, thus connecting it on a macrocosmic level with the higher nature of the spell. This helps to empower your act of magick. For Earth-related spells, bury the object in an area connected to your target. Spells related to the Element of Fire involve burning the links. Finally, for an Air-related spell, use steam or smoke.

Spell of the Witches' Ring

This is a simple spell designed to charge a ring that will serve as a protection. The Witches' ring is both a symbol and a tool of magick. As a symbol, it identifies the wearer as a practitioner of the Old Ways and declares one as a user of magick. As a tool, the ring connects the Witch to the metaphysical concepts whereby Witches weave their magick. The ring serves as a reminder to the Witch of the forces at hand and acts as a conduit to and from those occult forces readily available to the Witch. The preparation of the Witches' ring should begin two days before the first night of the Full Moon. Midnight is best, but 9:00 p.m. will do if necessary. The spell calls for a ring with a stone setting. Consult a table of occult correspondences for a stone that you wish to form an alignment with. Once you have the ring you desire, perform the following ritual:

1. Consecrate the ring to the Four Elements. To do this, simply prepare four bowls. Pour salt into one bowl and place smoking incense in another. In the third bowl, set a lighted red votive candle. Pour clean water into the last bowl. Then, touch the ring to each bowl saying:

> *"I consecrate thee by Earth (salt), Air (incense),*
> *Fire (votive candle), and Water (water bowl)."*

2. Pour a small amount of personal cologne in your burning dish. Light the fluid. Hold the ring over the flame, turning it, and chanting:

> *"I dedicate and consecrate this ring with a stone of (insert name of stone) and metal of (insert name of metal) to be a ring of witchery unto me with the powers of the Goddess three, the Lady of all Witchery, and as my word, so mote it be."*

3. Place an incense of the Moon in a bowl and light it. Set a bottle of Moon oil nearby. Center the ring over the incense, passing it through the smoke three times. Then, anoint the ring with the oil. Wrap the ring in a red cloth or tissue paper and leave it for three nights in a place where the Moon will shine on it each night at the same hour (at least one hour after sundown on an odd numbered hour.) Chant the following over the wrapped ring:

> *"Any and all who perfect an image of me,*
> *with my likeness or as a crude*
> *consecrated image to be me,*
> *to do me bodily harm or to injure me*
> *spiritually and try to take my breath away,*
> *to cause me to dwindle or pine, pine away to nothing,*
> *to wish evil upon me, to badger me with their anger*
> *or bad thoughts, by picture, image, or name,*
> *the ring of my Lady protects me,*

Spell of the Witches' Ring

metal and stone, flesh and bone,
safe forever in your powers,
free from evil, fear, or despair,
on the sender of the evil will rebound.
By the law of the Lady thrice crowned,
hearken all unto me,
as I speak, so mote it be."

Wear the ring whenever you are in a ritual setting or feel the need for protection. On the night of each Full Moon hereafter, anoint the ring again by rubbing a drop of oil on the stone. Then, raise the ring up toward the Moon and ask for blessings in the name of the Goddess.

Italian Witchcraft: The Survival of a Tradition

It has become popular in the Neo-Wiccan community these days to dismiss the Old Religion as a reconstructed system, or one which never existed but is a contemporary creation based upon ancient concepts. Some say that there is no evidence of a tie to any ancient and authentic way of worship. Others say that Witches have always been portrayed as evil in ancient times, and that there can be no similarity between ancient references to Witches and the image of Witches portrayed by Wicca today.

In this article, we will examine these issues and present some evidence that Witchcraft was indeed an ancient religion. We will show that Witches were not evil but simply maligned by a "solar" patriarchal society, which was opposed to the "lunar" matriarchal society.

In the book *Etruscan Magic & Occult Remedies*, author Charles Leland writes of his investigation into Italian Witchcraft: *"But I was much more astonished to find that in Tuscany, the most enlightened portion of Italy, under all Roman rule, an old Pagan faith, or something like it, has existed to a most extraordinary degree. For it is really not a mere chance survival of superstitions here and there, as in England or France, but a complete system, as this work will abundantly prove."* [29]

Leland later implies that he was taken into the Witches' community in his book *Legends of Florence*, in which he states: *"The Witches of Italy form a class who are the repositories of all the folklore; what is not at all generally known, they also keep as strict secrets an immense number of legends of their own, which have nothing in common with the nursery or popular tales, such as are commonly collected and published...Lady Vere de Vere, who has investigated Witchcraft as it exists in the Italian Tyrol, in an admirable article in La Rivista of Rome (June 1894) tells us that 'the Community of Italian Witches is regulated by laws, traditions, and customs of the most secret kind, possessing special recipes for sorcery' which is perfectly true. Having been free of the community for years, I can speak from experience. The more occult and singular of their secrets are naturally not of a nature to be published..."* [30]

What should be of particular interest here to modern Witches is Leland's (and Lady Vere de Vere's) use of the present tense when speaking of Witchcraft in their time. For those who believe that the Craft was invented by Gerald Gardner, bear in mind that this was written half a century before Gardner's books.

After consulting with Italian folklorist Lady Vere de Vere and Professor Milani (Director of the Archaeological Museum in Florence), Leland wrote in *Legends of Florence* (concerning Italian witchlore): *"That this is of great antiquity is clear, for out of this enchanted forest of Italian Witchcraft and mystical sorcery, there*

---

[29] Charles Godfrey Leland, *Etruscan Magic & Occult Remedies* (University Books, 1963) 9.

[30] Charles Godfrey Leland, *Legends of Florence: Collected from the People* (David Nutt, 1895) ix.

Italian Witchcraft: The Survival of a Tradition

never came anything great or small which was not at least of the Bronze Age, if not the neolithic age." [31]

In *Aradia: Gospel of the Witches*, Leland writes of the popular Christian image of the Witch, but goes on to say: *"But the Italian strega or sorceress is in certain respects a different character from these. In most cases she comes of a family in which her calling or art has been practiced for many generations...."* [32]

Again, we find Leland's use of the present tense when describing Witches in Italy circa 1880. Worthy of mention also in Leland's book is the story about the walnut Witches. Manuscripts from old Witch trials in Italy speak of this walnut tree, which (it is said) had always been there and was in leaf all year long. In Italy, legends were told for centuries of the great Witch gatherings in the town of Benevento at the site of an ancient walnut tree. In the year 662 CE, Saint Barbato converted the Pagan Duke of Benevento to Christianity, and had the tree cut down. The Witches replanted the walnut tree from seed, and legend says it still currently stands in Benevento. Bottles of Strega Liquore, manufactured in Benevento today, bear labels upon which appears the old walnut tree with a group of Witches and satyrs dancing around it.

There are several chapters in *Etruscan Magic & Occult Remedies* that support the existence of the Witch Cult in Italy during the nineteenth century and implications of its existence dating back to the days of antiquity. In Chapter Ten, Leland writes: *"...and it is interesting to know that in the city of Florence in the month of January, 1891, there were people who believe in a prehistoric Shamanism which is stronger and mightier than that of the Church. Ages*

---

31 Charles Godfrey Leland, *Legends of Florence: Collected from the People* (David Nutt, 1895) 252.

32 Charles Godfrey Leland, *Aradia: Gospel of the Witches* (David Nutt, 1899) vi.

have lapped over ages, the Etruscans and Sabine-Latin and Roman and Christian cults have succeeded one to the other, but through it all the Witch and wizard, humble and unnoted, have held their own." [33]

In Chapter Eight on the goddesses Diana and Herodias, Leeland writes: *"It is remarkable that while Witchcraft was regarded in later times among Northern races as a creation of Satan, it never lost in Italy a classic character. In this country the Witch is only a sorceress, and she is often a beneficent fairy. Her ruler is not the devil, but Diana...it is true enough that the monks imported and forced into popular Italian superstition strong infusions of the devil. Yet with all this, in the main, the real Italian Witch has nothing to do with Satan or a Christian hell and remains as of yore a daughter of Diana. There is something almost reviving or refreshing in the thought that there is one place in the world - and that in papal Italy itself — where the poison of diabolism did not utterly prevail."* [34]

So, what was the basis of the evil Witch image?

There are several ways to understand this distorted image, and we turn to the writings of the Roman poet Horace to begin our quest. In the *Epodes* of Horace, written around 30 BCE, he tells the tale of an Italian Witch named Canidia. Horace describes her as an old toothless hag with wild unkept hair, who casts evil spells upon those who offend her. Horace goes on to say that Proserpina and Diana grant power to Witches who worship them, and that Witches gather in secret to perform the mysteries associated with their worship. In Epode 5, we read: *"...Night and Diana, who com-*

---

33 Charles Godfrey Leland, *Etruscan Magic & Occult Remedies* (University Books, 1963) 196.

34 Charles Godfrey Leland, *Etruscan Magic & Occult Remedies* (University Books, 1963) 150.

Italian Witchcraft: The Survival of a Tradition

mand silence when secret mysteries are performed, now aid me; now turn your vengeance and influence against my enemies' house..."

In Epode 17, we find these words addressed to Canidia: *"Now already I yield to your mighty art, and suppliant beseech you by the realms of Proserpine, and by the powers of Diana, not to be provoked, and by your books of enchantments that are able to call down the fixed stars from heaven, Canidia, at length spare your magic words, and turn backward your swift wheel...* (Canidia replies) *"...must I, who can move waxen images and call down the Moon from the sky by my spells, who can raise the vaporous dead, and mix a draught of love lament the effect of my art, availing nothing upon you?"*

We know from the Roman writings that Proserpina and Diana were worshipped at night in secret ceremonies. Their worshippers gathered at night beneath the Full Moon and shunned the cities where the solar gods ruled. It is only logical that the city dwellers would fear them because they met in secret when "decent" people were already in bed. Out of their fear came the imaginings common to ignorance and prejudice. All unexplained ailments and disasters were in turn believed to come from these Witches who met in secret (for surely, they were plotting against the "good folk"). From generation to generation, prejudicial beliefs were passed on, becoming, in time, common knowledge. In the same way, prejudicial beliefs about minorities are kept alive today. One generation teaches another through comments and attitudes, and soon, distortion becomes fact. So, it is not surprising that the unsophisticated country-dwelling Pagan bore the image of the toothless evil hag, cursing the cattle and fields of her "good" neighbors. Since Witches were predominantly a matriarchy, the men who ruled the cities (and wrote the history) looked down upon them as rebellious and dangerous to the established order. In a patriarchal society, a woman who uses magick and worships in secret, having no need of patriarchal society or religion, can only be seen as an evil crazed woman.

In the traditional Halloween Witch image of Christian society, we are perhaps seeing the worst fears of a patriarchal society; a woman turned loose without the constraints of patriarchal rules or religious beliefs. In later times, the arrival of Christianity and its passion to convert Pagans, couple with its need to discredit Pagan ways to firmly establish Church doctrine led to the image of the evil Witch. The fact that some Witches went "renegade" to fight the Church, using Satan as the Church's powerful enemy, only reinforced the Church's belief in the evil nature of Witches. Most Witches chose not to denigrate the Old Ways and went underground, almost completely disappearing from history.

It is interesting to note, however, that there were good and evil Witches in Italy. In *Etruscan Magic & Occult Remedies*, Leland writes: "*True, there are Witches good and bad, but all whom I ever met belonged entirely to the buone (good). It was their rivals and enemies who were maladette streghe (evil Witches), et cetera, but the later I never met. We were all good.*"[35]

Even though the Church taught that all Witches were evil, their ancient cult continued through the centuries. Mircea Eliade wrote in his book *Occultism, Witchcraft and Cultural Fashions* concerning the existence and modern study of Witchcraft: "*It suffices to say that, as work progressed, the phenomenon of Witchcraft appeared more complex and consequently more difficult to explain by a single factor. Gradually it became evident that Witchcraft cannot be satisfactorily understood without the help of other disciplines, such as*

---

35 Charles Godfrey Leland, *Etruscan Magic & Occult Remedies* (University Books, 1963) 197.

Italian Witchcraft: The Survival of a Tradition

folklore, ethnology, sociology, psychology, and history of religions...for instance, even a rapid perusal of the Indian and Tibetan documents will convince an unprejudiced reader that European Witchcraft cannot be the creation of religious or political persecution or be a demonic sect devoted to Satan and the promotion of evil. As a matter of fact, all the features associated with European Witches are—with the exception of Satan and the Sabbath—claimed also by Indo-Tibetan yogis and magicians."[36]

Clearly, there is a common thread running through many ancient practices and beliefs. It is through our look back into time that we find the roots of Witchcraft. In his book *The World of Witches*, Julio Baroja writes of southern Europe: *"There seems to have been a flourishing Cult of Diana among European country people in the 5th and 6th Centuries (A.D.), and she was generally looked upon as a Goddess of the woods and fields, except by those trying to root out the cult, who thought she was a devil."*[37]

In the author's notes for Chapter Four, he adds that the cult also worshipped a male deity called Dianum. This may be of interest to modern writers on the Craft, such as Adian Kelly, who claim that Witches never worshipped Diana, or a God and Goddess consort, in ancient times.

In 906 CE, Regino of Prum wrote in his instructions to the Bishops of the Kingdoms of Italy concerning Witches: *"...they ride at night on certain beasts with Diana, goddess of the pagans, and a great multitude of women, that they cover great distances in the silence of the deepest night, that they obey the orders of the goddess...by speaking of their visions (they) gain new followers for the Society of Diana...."*

---

36   Mircea Eliade, *Occultism, Witchcraft, and Cultural Fashions: Essays in Comparative Religion* (University of Chicago Press, 2012) 71.

37   Julio C. Baroja, *The World of the Witches* (Phoenix Press, 2001).

71

Raven's Call

It is interesting to note that the label "Society of Diana" mentioned by Regino in 906 CE continues to be associated with Witches throughout the centuries in Italy, as recorded in Witch trials by the Italian Inquisition. It appears with greater frequency during the late 1300s and into the late 1400s in Italian Witch trials. A brief chronology follows to summarize this unbroken chain of Italian Witchcraft through the centuries:

- **30 CE:** Roman poet Horace in his *Epodes* associates Witches with the goddess Diana in a mystery cult.
- **314 CE:** Council of Ancyra labels Witches as heretics who believe that they belong to a "Society of Diana." Council concludes that they are deceived by Satan.
- **662 CE:** Saint Barbato converts Romuald (Duke of Benevento) to Christianity. On Saint Barbato's bidding, Romuald has the "Witches' walnut tree" cut down. This walnut tree was the gathering place of Witches, well known in the region. In 680 CE, Saint Barbato attended the Council of Constantinople, where he spoke out against the "Witches of Benevento."
- **906 CE:** Regino of Prum in his instructions to the bishops claims that Pagans worship Diana in a cult called the "Society of Diana."
- **1006 CE:** Nineteenth book of the *Decretum* (entitled "Corrector") associates the worship of Diana with the common Pagan folk.
- **1280 CE:** Diocesan Council of Conserans associates the "Witch Cult" with the worship of a Pagan goddess.
- **1310 CE:** Council of Trier associates Witches with the goddess Diana (and Herodias).
- **1313 CE:** Giovanni de Matoclis writes in his *Historia Imperiales* that many lay people believe in a nocturnal society headed by a queen they call Diana.

- **1390 CE:** A woman is tried by the Milanese Inquisition for belonging to the "Society of Diana;" she confessed to worshipping the "goddess of night" and stated that Diana bestowed blessings upon her.
- **1457 CE:** Three women tried in Bressanone confessed that they belonged to the "Society of Diana" (as recorded by Nicholas of Cus).
- **1526 CE:** Judge Paulus Grillandus writes of Witches in the town of Benevento who worship a goddess at the site of an old walnut tree.
- **1576 CE:** Bartolo Spina consolidates information from confessions in *Quaestio de strigibus*, which presents Witches gathering at night to worship Diana and dealing with night spirits.
- **1647 CE:** Pietro Piperno writes in *De Nuce Maga Beneventana* and *De Effectibus Magicis* of a woman named Violanta who confessed to worshipping Diana at the site of an old walnut tree in the town of Benevento.
- **1749 CE:** Girloamo Tartarotti associates the Witch Cult with the ancient Cult of Diana in his book *Del Congresso Notturno Delle Lammie*.
- **1890 CE:** Charles Leland associates the Witch Cult with the goddess Diana and as a survival of the ancient ways in his books: *Etruscan Magic & Occult Remedies*, *Legends of Florence*, and *Aradia: Gospel of the Witches*.

Professor Carlo Ginzburg, author of *The Night Battles: Witchcraft and Agrarian Cults in the Sixteenth and Seventeenth Centuries* and *Ecstasies: Deciphering the Witches' Sabbath*, presents compelling evidence of Witchcraft as the survival of a hidden shamanistic culture that flourished across the European continent and in England for thousands of years. In *Ecstasies*, Ginzburg presents evidence which supports the antiquity of the Witch Cult. Although stuck with the Christian image of evil Witches, he possessed the knowledge of pre-Christian European religion, which he believed connected Witches to an ancient fertility cult that was once prevalent across central Europe.

Ginzburg has an interesting approach to the study of Witchcraft. Some scholars who study Witchcraft look at the trial transcripts and dismiss the statements as fantasy, concluding that such a cult never existed, but was due to some kind of hysteria. Ginzburg looks at the material as though the statements indicate what the people believed and then explores why they would have believed themselves to have participated in such events. Through this line of investigation emerges an ancient shamanistic practice involving organic hallucinogens, which were employed to send the practitioners off into other realms of consciousness.

This, of course, resulted in the fantastic stories of flight, mythical creatures, orgies, and wild Sabbats (not to mention whatever may have been contributed to the trial transcripts by the Inquisition for its own agenda). Let us now examine the internal mechanism for the survival in Italian Witchcraft.

The Veglia, Sacred Fire, and Italian Witchcraft

In the book *Folklore by the Fireside: Text and Context of the Tuscan Veglia*, professor of anthropology Alessandro Falassi explores the Italian custom known as the *veglia* (pronounced vay-yah). The word *veglia* is roughly translatable as "wake" and is like the Latin word *vigilia*, meaning "to stay awake" during the usual hours of sleep (a vigil). In Italy, the veglia has always been the occasion in which societal rules and values were discussed and transmitted in rural Tuscany. Folklore has provided for centuries the means and messages of such crucial communicative events. Falassi describes the scene in which Italian peasants once returned from the fields at sunset and gathered before the fireplace. Here, they would first tell fairy tales to children, which contained various messages and morals intended to assimilate the child into their community. Next, the older children were told stories of their family members and ancestors to establish a sense of who they were and who they had been. Lastly, they spoke of their religious beliefs and customs to preserve their traditions. It is because of the traditions like the veglia that so much of hereditary Italian Witchcraft has survived and been passed on. Alessandro Falassi writes of the veglia:

"...the word and the custom that surrounds it have an old-fashioned ring to Tuscans today. Yet these fireside evenings and their homespun performances are not so far removed from contemporary people's experience, for it is only in the last decade or so that the occasion has lost its vitality... The veglia has lasted over 500 years without losing its function or meaning." [38]

To attend a veglia, one traditionally had to be a member of the family, or "of the blood," as they would say. Other participants in the veglia could be relatives or those related through marriage. Throughout the Middle Ages, the veglia was held between the fall and winter when crops were sewn and Lent was observed, even though the common rituals were performed all year.

The fireside hearth was the center of the Italian Pagan's home, and has maintained its place for centuries. The family and the fireplace belonged to the mother of the home, and it was she who tended the fire. As Falassi says: *"...it was she who nurtured and protected the spark by which life could be lived, measured and regulated...it was the mother of the house who stooped in front of the andirons to blow on the fire to communicate by contagious magick her soul, the vital breath that popular belief considered to be exactly fire. She was the one to make it start...it was always she who regulated the fire's intensity, adding or removing pieces with the poker of the tongs, according to necessity."* [39]

In the center of the fireplace sat the "fire stone," a fireproof slab over which the fire burned. In a folklore belief, the umbilical cords of the children were placed beneath the stone to ensure the family's unity. This usage suggests that the fire stone was an

---

38 Alessandro Falassi, *Folklore by the Fireside: Text and Context of the Tuscan Veglia* (University of Texas Press, 1980) 248.

39 Alessandro Falassi, *Folklore by the Fireside: Text and Context of the Tuscan Veglia* (University of Texas Press, 1980) 2.

The Veglia, Sacred Fire, and Italian Witchcraft

important element in the veglia family gatherings. Concerning the fire stone, Falassi writes:

"Above it the fire burned perennially; under it they laid a votive offering to obtain the grace of union and family continuity—all of this qualified it as a functional equivalent of the altar in the family context. Moreover, the fire of the fireplace, like that of the religious ritual, represented an element of purification through the separation of the substance: the smoke had to rise to the top, ad astra, through the chimney. If it stayed low, or if it was forced back by the wind, it brought bad luck and became one of the elements that chased man from the house. The cinders, product of transformation more than discarded material, returned back to the animal and vegetable world. Because they came from the fire, they remained a fecundative clement: 'The cinders are the honor of the fire. The fire burned on the slab of the fireplace remained as a pure element and continually purified itself.'" [40]

The main substance of the fire at the veglia was the burning *ceppo,* or "log." This log always came from the part of the tree closest to the roots, connecting the log symbolically to family roots. Ceppo is also used in Italian to refer to a "group of houses" or a "family." The log was the symbol of marriage in Roman times, and the woman symbolized the tree of life, so the symbolism of the veglia is likely ancient.

The fireplace was the center of the house, providing heat and light to prepare food. It was the point at which Nature merged with human culture. Here also hung the items common to domestic family life, but which were also symbols of the generative act of life and of the family. The female symbols were the kettle, the chimney, and the chain, symbolizing the womb, the vaginal passage,

---

40 Alessandro Falassi, *Folklore by the Fireside: Text and Context of the Tuscan Veglia* (University of Texas Press, 1980) 26.

and the unifying principle of family. The male symbols were the fire poker, the tongs (phallic representations), and the fire itself, of which Falassi writes: *"Fire in native as well as psychoanalytic imagery represents the principle of male sexuality; the combustion represents and imitates both the sexual and the generative act: the sparks, the male seeds."* [41]

It was here that the family gathered to hear the old stories told and retold. The fire that illuminated the narrator served as the explanatory principle and signifier of both magickal transformation and the metaphysics of the family. It only made sense that this would be the place where family values and worldviews would be shared amongst those of the same blood. It was here that hereditary Witches were kept bound from one generation to the next through family tales of bloodlines and religious beliefs, mixed with folklore and legend.

The earliest references to the veglia in Italian literature date from the 1400s, although certainly this was a much older practice. In the Italian Tradition, gatherings at the time of the Full Moon are referred to as the *veglione* (pronounced *vay-yoe-nay*), although the slang term *tregua* (*tray-gwah*) is more commonly used, which means "respite."

The root word of veglione is clearly veglia. Veglione means "to dance all night," and today is the name of a traditional Italian dance. The ritual gathering at the time of Full Moon was a respite from the burdens of daily work and drudgery for the Pagan peasants of old Italy; hence the slang word "tregua."

This was also true of the yearly celebrations of the great festivals, many of which were adopted and altered by the Church,

---

41   Ibid.

making it easier for the Pagans to celebrate in the open under the guise of Christian worship. Open worship of the saints became a useful cover for the worship of the old gods, as Witches adapted to the ruling class of the period. Some modern Italian Witches see Catholics as Pagans who accept Christ as Divine, and certainly many aspects of Italian Paganism have survived in Roman Catholicism. Clearly, Mary has similar qualities to a goddess, the "Mother of God," and Jesus contains elements of the Slain God, born at the winter solstice, which are linked to themes of resurrection, and maintain the ancient cycle of the Green Man.

The fire of the veglia is still kindled today by Italian Witches in the form of the "spirit flame," which burns upon the altar. Placed directly in the center of the altar is a bowl that holds the blue flame, symbolizing the presence of the ancient spirit of the Old Ways. In a real sense, this is more than a symbol, as Italian Witches invoke the ancient ones directly within the flame and draw their power from divine fire. Fire is one of the most ancient forms of divinity and a common focus in most ancient cultures.

In *The Golden Bough*, James Frazer makes reference to the divine fire at the sanctuary of Diana in Lake Nemi: *"For the perpetual holy fires of the Aryans in Europe appear to have been commonly kindled and fed with oak-wood, and in Rome itself, not many miles from Nemi, the fuel of the vestal fire consisted of oaken sticks or logs as has been proven by a microscopic analysis of the charred embers of the Vestal fire...if Diana was a queen of the woods in general, she was at Nemi a goddess of the oak in particular. In the first place, she bore the title of Vesta, and as such presided over a perpetual fire, which we have seen reason to believe was fed with oakwood. But a goddess of fire is not far removed from a goddess of the fuel which burns in the fire; primitive thought perhaps drew no sharp line of distinction between the blaze and the wood that blazes."*[42]

Here again we see the ancient connection between the log, fire, and the female spirit (which is the setting for the veglia).

Literally, it was "folklore by the fireplace" that preserved so much of Italian Witchcraft, and as Falassi wrote, *"folklore does not exist in a timeless dimension, but rather in a concrete process that is part of a ritual meeting held in the heart of a cultural group, definite in time and space."* [43] Fortunately, the persecution of Witches in Italy began almost one hundred years later than it did in Northern Europe, and even then, the local village Witch was generally tolerated, as the Church hunted mainly for organized groups. Thankfully, the persecution of Italian Witches was not as fierce in Italy, although many Witches (and non-Witches) were burned in its war against religious freedom. This fact, along with the tradition of the veglia, helped many family traditions survive centuries of persecution that severely fragmented so many of the Witch traditions of Northern Europe.

In a sense, these writings are a veglia, preserving the old legends and stories, whispers of one generation to the next. Perhaps someone out there sits before a fireplace and reads this quaint and curious volume of forgotten lore. So, I close with these final words from Falassi: *"The old woman placed herself in the center, inside the fireplace, at the fireplace, that is, in direct contact with the fire, which together with herself became an evocator and operator of images, mediator of the past and present, now and once upon a time, real truth and imagined truth, good and bad. Through the reverie in*

---

42   Frazer, James, *The Golden Bough: A Study in Magic and Religion* (Oxford University Press, 1998) 14.

43   Alessandro Falassi, *Folklore by the Fireside: Text and Context of the Tuscan Veglia* (University of Texas Press, 1980) 248.

the ambiguous light and dark, the narrator and her familiar public once again found, by renewing it, a primary and most cultural function of mankind: storytelling." [44]

---

[44] Alessandro Falassi, *Folklore by the Fireside: Text and Context of the Tuscan Veglia* (University of Texas Press, 1980) 28.

Lupercus: Wolf God of Winter

Probably one of the oldest and yet most confusing aspects of Aridian Witchcraft is the god form known as Lupercus, the Wolf God of Winter. Traditionally, he is known as the Great Golden Wolf who drives away the wolves of night, and in this form, we can clearly see the solar aspect connected to Lupercus. In fact, it is Lupercus who is born at winter solstice and reaches puberty on his ritual day, which occurs on February 2nd, or *Candelora*, as it is popularly known in Italy.

In ancient Rome, the Lupercalia was an important religious festival celebrated on February 15th near the Lupercal, which was a cave in the Palatine Hill. According to Roman mythology, a wolf nursed the infant twins Romulus and Remus in this cave. The festival included banquets, dancing, and sacrifices of a goat and a dog. The goat and the dog are domesticated images of the stag and the wolf, transformed by an agricultural society. Whips were made of the goat hide, which were later used by the priests of Lupercus (known as the *Luperci*). During those times, it was customary for women who yearned for pregnancy to be pursued and struck with a lash made from goat's hide by the Luperci. This practice was believed to impart the fertile essence of the goat to the woman.

Some scholars believe that there was no god named Lupercus worshipped at these rites, but instead claim they were held in honor of Faunus, the Roman version of Pan. In the book *Roman and European Mythologies* compiled by Yves Bonnefoy, we find these interesting passages: *"Uncertainty also arises from the fact that the association of Faunus with the Cult of the Lupercalia, undoubtedly the most archaic of Roman cults, is relatively recent...in fact, the name of this festival bears only a semantic correspondence to Lupercal, which designates the cave of the she-wolf and the Luperci, the officials of this truly savage brotherhood' who on February 15th ran around the Palatine as if to trace a Circle of Magic protection...Furthermore, these Luperci are nearly naked, wearing only a loincloth... Clearly these Luperci, since they are divided into two groups, the Quintales (who are connected with Romulus) and the Fabiani (who are connected with Remus) are situated at a stage before civilization."* [45]

The she-wolf was an Etruscan symbol to which the Romans added Romulus and Remus; an ancient memory from where Rome had "suckled" its strength and grew to greatness. It is no mere coincidence that the standard bearers of the Roman army (the strength of Rome) wore wolf headdresses into battle. Lycisca, the wolf goddess, was also the wife of Lupercus. No offspring are ever mentioned in their mythos. In the book *The Cult of Pan in Ancient Greece* by Philippe Borgeaud, Pan (Faunus in Roman mythology) is linked with wolves, and Faunus is associated with the Lupercalia. Borgeaud alludes to the mythical Lyssa, implying that etymologically, Lyssa derives its meaning from "she-wolf," specifically referring to her ability to transform someone into a

---

45 Yves Bonnefoy, *Roman and European Mythologies* (University of Chicago Press, 1992) 126.

Lupercus: Wolf God of Winter

wolf. It may be that Lyssa and Lycisca are one and the same, or at least closely linked.

In the mythos, the Sun descends into the Underworld at night and returns to the Earth each morning, gathering the souls of those who died for their journey to the Realm of the Dead. This deity is Lupercus, the Great Golden Wolf.

Borgeaud states that the god Pan *"shares the power with Lyssa."* This seems to explain the appearance of Pan on Italian vases, representing the death of Actaeon. In the Aridian Tradition, Actaeon is the stag god of the forest at Nemi in Italy. The popular myth of Actaeon tells the tale of how he was transformed into a stag while hunting, and that his dogs went mad and turned on him. In his book, Borgeaud writes: *"Pan, grandson of Lykaon the wolf-man, is evidently a specialist in such metamorphoses...we have seen the god transform the shepherds and goatherds into wolves and savage dogs..."*[46]

This passage suggests Faunus is associated with the wolf-oriented Lupercalia and explains why goats and dogs appear in the rite. Certainly, the fact that his grandfather Lykaon was a "wolf-man" makes one wonder.

In the mythology of the Triad Witch Clans of Italy, there are two gods born at the winter solstice (fathered by Janus); they are fraternal twin brothers separated at birth by an abductor who flees with Cern, the stag god. It is probable that Romulus and Remus may also serve as symbolic recollections of this much older legend. They likely represent the mythos of the gods associated with the waxing and waning year, similar to Lupercus and Cern in the Witch Clans of the Triad Tradition.

---

46 Phillip Borgeaud, *The Cult of Pan in Ancient Greece* (University of Chicago Press, 1988) 123.

One wonders whether the Luperci, divided into groups associated with Romulus and with Remus, may relate to the Benandanti and Malandanti cults, which fought ritual battles over the crops and herds and represented the waxing and waning powers of the year.

The ritual of Lupercus in the Aridian Tradition is a rite of purification and liberation. Participants are blessed and purified through the ancient ways after a ritual drama play, and the rite ends in an atavistic experience wherein coven members "transform" into wolves; not literally, of course, but spiritually. This is directed and overseen by the priest of the circle, who represents one of the ancient Luperci. This aspect of the rite reflects the ancient practice of the Luperci introducing hallucinogens into their celebrations, carefully monitoring the experiences of those who participated in the ritual. The purpose of this transformation was to free the untamed aspect of the individual and thus release the atavistic power within. This was the essence of "shapeshifting," and it may have contributed to later werewolf legends.

In the mythos of Lupercus, he is given twelve labors to perform to prove himself worthy as the new Sun god. The labors represent the passage of the Sun through the twelve zodiac signs, which completes the cycle of one year. On the spring equinox, while hunting a deer, he is struck by a bolt of lightning, and seemingly perishes. The next morning, he rises from the Underworld as the Sun. Having learned of his brother Lupercus who ascended and left his earthly throne void, Cern becomes the god of this world and reigns in his place. The only physical remains of Lupercus is his wolf skin, which is found by another hunter in the forest. The pelt turns out to be magickal and has the power to transform men into wolves. The first man to wear the wolf pelt of Lupercus became a priest of the god and founded the society of the Luperci.

Lupercus: Wolf God of Winter

Lupercus represents winter, the waning season of the year (even though he is a sun god). His brother Cern, the Stag God of the Forest, represents the waxing year. In this mythos, we find the rivalry of winter and summer, opposing forces and yet related "brothers," necessary to balance the scheme of Nature. Lupercus is slain during the hunt, in which Cern is the hunted. He is slain by a centaur who is given a bolt of lightning for his bow by Dianus (having been persuaded by his sister Diana). Cern is later slain as well, but on the autumn equinox by Mars during another hunting incident. It is interesting to note that the centaur in the constellation Centaurus is aiming a bow at the constellation Lupus, the wolf. In mythology, the Centaur was beloved by Apollo and Diana, who instructed him in many of the ancient arts. Diana and the stag are strongly associated in the Witch Cult, and, in her classic Roman statue, she is portrayed standing with a stag. It's also interesting to observe that the wolf held sacred status to Mars, possibly hinting at a form of "vengeance" in the myth of Cern.

The story of Lupercus is a tale of our own journey and struggle with our higher and lower natures. We find the journey of our own soul in the cycle of the Sun god: born in darkness, growing into the fullness of light, slain, and then descending back into darkness, only to be reborn again. It is a myth of transformation, renewal, challenge, and accomplishment. In the ritual of Lupercus, we release the wolf within us; that which is untamed and unowned (even by ourselves). Through this purging of the contaminations of modern life and the imposed restrictions of an oppressive society, we realign ourselves to the nature within, and, out of this, we refocus upon our journey towards enlightenment. In this hunt for ourselves, we are "struck by lightning" and are transformed into a new light.

The Saturnalia

In ancient Rome, a festival in December known as the Saturnalia was a popular observance. It is in this celebration from the days of antiquity that we find a character titled the Lord of Misrule. This mythic rite was to have more influence upon later European customs than perhaps any other. In the pre-Republican calendar, the festival started on December 17th and usually ran for several days, ending on the winter solstice. Bonfires blazed during this time, and the celebration was marked by orgies, carnivals, and gift giving.

Masters and slaves changed places, and the world was turned upside down for a short period. All of this was overseen by the Lord of Misrule. The Saturnalian revelries and orgies were not tamed until the fourteenth century, when the Catholic Church had enough power to finally exert its authority over both the government and the people.

The person chosen to play the Lord of Misrule had to be a young, strong, and virile male. For thirty days prior to the festival, he was allowed to indulge himself in any and all pleasures as he pleased. He was dressed in royal robes and was treated like a king. This young man represented the god Saturn, in whose honor the festival was originated. The Romans considered Saturn to be a god of cultivated fields and sprouting seed; according to legend, the Lord of Misrule was the first king of Latium and was the first to introduce agriculture. James Frazer in *The Golden Bough* states he was slain upon the altar of Saturn by having his throat cut at the end of the festival. His blood was then given to the fields, so that his vitality passed into the soil, revitalizing the life within the earth and ensuring a bountiful harvest for the next year. In the classical period of Horace and Tacitus, this king was a buffoon figure, but in earlier times, he was the sacrificial king.

James Frazer writes: *"We can hardly doubt that in the King of the Saturnalia at Rome, as he is depicted by classical writers, we can see only a feeble emasculated copy of that original, whose strong features have been fortunately preserved for us by the obscure author of the Martyrdom of St. Dasius. In other words, the martyrologist's account of the Saturnalia agrees so closely with the accounts of similar rites elsewhere which could not possibly have been known to him, that the substantial accuracy of his description may be regarded as established; and further, since the custom of putting a mock king to death as a representative of a god cannot have grown out of a practice of appointing him to preside over a holiday revel..."* [47]

In Italy, the winter festival of "Carnevale" (the Carnival) closely resembles the revels of the Saturnalia, except for the literal slaying of the king, of course. Frazer writes: *"The resemblance between the Saturnalia of ancient and the Carnival of modern Italy has often been remarked, but in the light of all the facts that have come before us, we may well ask whether the resemblance does not amount to identity. We have seen that in Italy, Spain and France, that is, in the countries where the influence of Rome has been the deepest and*

---

47 James Frazer, *The Golden Bough: A Study in Magic and Religion* (Oxford University Press, 1998) 632.

The Saturnalia

most lasting, a conspicuous feature of the Carnival is a burlesque figure personifying the festive season, which after a short career of glory and dissipation is publicly shot, burnt, or otherwise destroyed, to the feigned grief or genuine delight of the populace. If the view here suggested of the Carnival is correct, this grotesque personage is no other than a direct successor of the old king of the Saturnalia..." [48]

In ancient Rome, a pig was sacrificed at the Saturnalia. In later times, this was substituted with a trickster character and, in more recent times, by a great buffoon who ruled as the King of the Carnival. This character was carried about upon a throne as he reclined, wearing the costume of a pig.

Traditionally, a fava bean was baked into a focaccia cake, and the contestant who found the bean became the Lord of Misrule. The custom of placing a fava bean in a focaccia cake still takes place at Carnival in Italy, along with many tamed versions of the original revels of the Roman Saturnalia. J.C. Cooper, in his book *The Aquarian Dictionary of Festivals*, comments on the ancient and modern associations of the Saturnalia: *"The characteristics of this time passed from Rome into Europe, persisting into medieval times, having also a Lord of Misrule."* [49] Frazer goes into greater depth of connection in *The Golden Bough*, where he associates the Lord of Misrule with The King of the Woods, who ruled in the sanctuary of Diana at Lake Nemi in Italy. Frazer's book deals with the Slain God mythos, which is an integral part of the Old Religion. In *The Golden Bough*, we find these words from Frazer: *"We may conclude with a fair degree of probability that if the King of the Wood*

---

48 James Frazer, *The Golden Bough: A Study in Magic and Religion* (Oxford University Press, 1998) 285.

49 J. C. Cooper, *The Aquarian Dictionary of Festivals* (Wildside Press, LLC, 1990).

Raven's Call

at Aricia lived and died as an incarnation of a sylvan deity, he had of old a parallel at Rome in the men who, year by year, were slain in the character of King Saturn, the god of the sown and sprouting seed." [50]

Clearly, we can see here the Slain God mythos of the Western Mystery Tradition; the Lord of the Vegetation (formerly the Lord of the Woods) sacrificed into the harvest. It is interesting to note that yet another northern European Craft mythos originated in Italy.

---

[50] James Frazer, *The Golden Bough: A Study in Magic and Religion* (Oxford University Press, 1998) 493.

The Benandanti

In sixteenth-century Italy, the Church encountered an ancient society which called itself the Benandanti. From the records of the Inquisition, the Benandanti and their beliefs are described. Professor Carlo Ginzburg recorded much about the Benandanti in his book *The Night Battles: Witchcraft and Agrarian Cults in the 16th and 17th Centuries*. Although interpreted through the eyes of the Christian Church, the "confessions" of the Benandanti contain a great deal of information confirming the existence and theology of the Witch Cult as a surviving tradition from pre-Christian European roots. In the foreword to Ginzburg's book, we find these statements:

"Some time in the late 16th Century the attention of a perplexed Church was drawn to the prevalence of a curious practice in the region of the Friuli, where German, Italian and Slav customs meet.... Carlo Ginzburg argues that theirs was a fertility ritual once widespread throughout central Europe, but by this period perhaps flourishing only in marginal regions such as the Friuli (and Lithuania, whence a strictly similar institution of benevolent werewolves is recorded from the late 17th Century), and suggests Slav or even Ural-Altaic influences, which must be left to the judgment of experts in popular religion."[51]

---

51   Carlo Ginzburg, *The Night Battles: Witchcraft & Agrarian Cults in the Sixteenth & Seventeenth Centuries* (Routledge & Kegan Paul, 1983) ix.

On March 21, 1575, a priest named Don Bartolomeo Sgabarizza appeared before Monsignor Jacopo Maracco at the Monastery of San Francisco di Cividale with an amazing account of a local practice. He related the story of a man named Paolo Gasparutto who had a reputation as a healer (more so of enchantments). Upon questioning, Paolo admitted that he belonged to a society called the Benandanti ("good-doers"). He then revealed that the Benandanti would fall into trances on certain nights (called the Ember Days) and that their souls would leave their bodies. Then, they engaged in ritual combat with the Malandanti (evil-doers) over the fate of the harvest. The Malandanti fought with sorghum stalks, and the Benandanti fought with stalks of fennel in a ritual joust. In a recorded "confession" by a man named Battista Moduco, we find these words:

"In the fighting that we do, one time we fight over the wheat and all the other grains, another time over the livestock, and at other times over the vineyards. And so, on four occasions we fight over all the fruits of the earth and for those things won by the Benandanti that year there is abundance."

With continued discoveries and trial transcripts spanning over 100 years in the archives of the Inquisition, it is clear the Benandanti existed. The information is consistent and does not seem to be designed by the inquisitors, as it rarely plays into the hands of the Christian Church in its attack upon the Old Religion. In fact, the Benandanti at first denied practicing Witchcraft, insisting that they were an army for Christ in the war against Evil. Obviously, it would have been dangerous and foolish to profess oneself as a "good Witch." They gave accounts of carrying white banners bearing a gilded lion into battle and described the Malandanti banner as red, bearing four black angels. In time, the confessions begin to contain contradictions, and eventually, the Benandanti

The Benandanti

confessions were seen as evidence of Witchcraft; nevertheless, they asserted they fought on the side of Good against evil Witches.

The background information which the trial transcripts contain is particularly interesting to modern Witches, as they support to the long-claimed practices of Wicca and Witchcraft. We have already mentioned that the Benandanti described "leaving the body" (astral projection), but there are other aspects to their practices which connect to the Old Religion as well. In the confessions of Paolo Gasparutto and Battista Maduco, we find the Benandanti and the Malandanti (referred to as Witches in their confessions) gathered for seasonal rites associated with the fertility of crops and animals. They held feasts and played games, performed marriages, and danced. These all speak to an existing community, with structured practices and customs. Since marriages were performed at these gatherings, we can assume that the society had priests and priestesses to perform the rites, and that a marriage rite would seemingly imply the existence of a religious or spiritual tradition.

Professor Ginzburg relates the rites of the Benandanti to an older tradition, which he believes was once widespread throughout Europe. Ginzburg writes: *"It may be supposed that this combat re-enacted, and to a certain extent rationalized, an older fertility rite in which two groups of youths, respectively impersonating demons favorable to fertility and the maleficent ones of destruction, symbolically flayed their loins with stalks of fennel and sorghum to stimulate their own reproductive capacity, and by analogy, the fertility of the fields of the community. Gradually the rite may have come to be represented as an actual combat, and from the uncertain outcome of the struggler between the two opposed bands would magically defend the fertility of the land and the fate of the harvests. At a later state these rites would cease to be practiced openly and would exist precariously, between the dreamlike*

Raven's Call

and the hallucinatory, in any case on a purely internal emotional plane — and yet without quite sliding into mere individual fantasizing."[52]

Ginzburg goes on to associate the struggle between the Benandanti and the Malandanti as an analogy of the rites of contest between the waxing and waning year. The use of fennel and sorghum represent the plants of winter and summer and are symbols of conflict and resolution. Here, we see not only the ancient passing of power in a seasonal sense, but also the classic struggle of good against evil.

Stories abound of villages during the Middle Ages whose people burned evil effigies and symbolically drove off evil doers with rods and staffs beyond the village's boundaries. Many of these accounts can be found in *The Golden Bough* by James Frazer and many other works.

The Benandanti fought against negative and destructive thought-forms and cleansed the collective consciousness of their communities. Theirs was a battle against evil personified in a war between the armies of light and darkness. It might not be a bad idea for Witches today to clear some garden space for a bit of fennel sometime soon.

---

52   Carlo Ginzburg, *The Night Battles: Witchcraft & Agrarian Cults in the Sixteenth & Seventeenth Centuries* (Routledge & Kegan Paul, 1983) 24.

The Spirit Blade

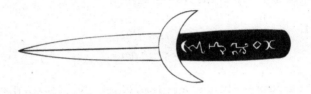

One of the most common tools associated with the practice of the Craft today is the athame (or spirit blade, as it is called in the Aridian Tradition). This article will cover the ritual preparation for the knife as performed in the Nemaic System of Witchcraft. The Nemaic System was developed by me in 1980 and is based upon the old Italian tradition. I first presented the System in my books, *The Book of Ways, Volume I and Volume II*. Please bear in mind that this technique is an eclectic modern work, yet based upon an old tradition.

Preparation

Three nights before the Moon is full (the third night being the Full Moon), dig a small hole as deep as your hand in the earth. Then, take equal portions (about a handful) of grounded rue, vervain, and angelica. Add them to the soil to the hole and mix together. Replace the soil and leave it until the night of the Full Moon.

On the night of the Full Moon, boil water (about 8 ounces) and add three pinches of salt. Then, go out to the hole and slowly pour the boiled water upon it. Next, mark a triangle around the hole, and then place nine drops of liquid camphor (Campho-Phenique will do, in a pinch) directly upon the center of the hole. At this point, grasp the dagger in both hands, blade pointing down, and raise your arms up to the Moon, saying:

*"O Great Tana,
bless me with power."*

Then, push the blade into the soil (directly center in the hole) up to the handle base. Next, draw power down from the Moon, using the following procedure.

Kneel before the Moon, hands upon thighs, and say:

*"At will, I make swift streams retire
to their fountains,
whilst their banks admire;
sea toss and smooth;
clear clouds with clouds deform.
With spells and charms
I break the Viper's jaw,
cleave solid rocks,
oaks from their seizures draw,
whole woods remove,
the lofty mountains shake,*

The Spirit Blade

*Earth for to groan,
and ghosts from graves awake,
and Thee, O Moon, I draw...."*

(As you begin the last verse, raise your left hand and "cup" the Moon.)

Then, quickly grasp your hand, seemingly closing the Moon within your palm. Do not look up at this point, but bring your closed hand down (as if drawing or pulling) and grasp the knife handle. Next, place your right hand firmly over your left and concentrate upon the knife, imagining it glowing with power. After a few minutes, remove the knife from the soil and clean it off with a white cloth. The knife is then ready for the symbols to be placed upon the handle. All that remains is to charge the knife with the Four Elements and to dedicate it to the service of Tana.

The Stag & The Wolf

In the Old Religion of Italy, there are three aspects of the God. In these aspects, we find the connections of deity within the physical world. The three titles are the Hooded One, the Horned One, and the Old One. In many traditions, the Hooded One is referred to as the Green Man or Jack-in-the-Green. He is covered in foilage or hooded in green. The Horned One is a stag-horned deity and is the god of the forests or of the wild. The Old One is the sage or elder.

According to archaeologist Miranda Green, the earliest known representation of the stag-horned god appears on a rock carving in Val Camonica, Italy, dating back to the fourth century BCE. In this carving, he appears as a human dressed in a long robe, standing with his arms uplifted, and a pair of antlers upon his head. In Green's book *Symbol and Image in Celtic Religious Art*, Green shares images of the engravings from the pre-historic period at Trois-Freres, which depicts humans dressed in animal skins (including a stag disguise) engaged in hunting and ceremonial acts. While these pre-historic carvings picture a human disguised as a stag, the carving in Italy I believe may portray the stag itself as a deity

Raven's Call

The three aspects of the god evolved from the merging of a hunter-gatherer society and agricultural community. The Hooded One was connected with crops and came after the Stag God as his son. The hunter-gatherer existed long before agriculture, and therefore the animal spirit was valued before the plant spirit. As humankind grew spiritually, the concept of the Old One was born. This was the human representation of deity; the god man.

Other aspects of the God are variations of these three basic concepts. The Trickster, for example, is associated with the Hooded One. We see this in the poem *Sir Gawain and the Green Knight*, who tricked Gawain, and again during the Saturnalia, when the Lord of Misrule was sacrificed. In the Italian Tradition, the Raven (a renown trickster) is associated with the Hooded One in his role as the Guardian of the Grove. The common image of the goat-foot god, or Pan-like god, is merely a domesticated version of the Stag God of the Forest. As humankind began farming, domesticated animals became more important than hunted animals, and the symbolism began to change. Gods like Pan or Faunus were simply the Stag God of the Forest as seen by agricultural communities, which valued domesticated animals more than wild animals of the forest. The winter months brought on the wolves who preyed upon both domesticated and wild animals.

Wolves were seen as symbols of the power of winter. Their connection with the Stag God of the Forest (the Hunted and the Hunter) lay deep in the memories of early humankind. Thus, the Stag God came to symbolize the waxing year, and the Wolf God came to represent the waning year. This Wolf God was known as Lupercus, or sometimes Lupus.

The Stag and the Wolf God originate in the Witch Cult of antiquity. An early Etruscan image on a vase from the sixth

The Stag & The Wolf

century BCE shows the Goddess holding a wolf and a stag. This is unsurprising, for Italian Witchcraft has its roots in Tuscany, which is where the Etruscan civilization once stood.

The Wolf, the "Howler of the Night," was the Goddess's principal cult animal. Its importance in the religion of Old Europe can be found in many figurines and vessels depicting them. Wolves were sacred to the Moon Goddess, and the lunar nature is stressed by the crescents which appear along with their images on ancient artifacts. Today, the image of the goddess Diana is often depicted in art accompanied with hunting dogs, but the earliest statues of Diana show her with a stag. Through Diana, we discover the seasons of the stag and of the wolf.

The season of the waxing year is symbolized by the cycle of regeneration and growth of the stag's antlers. Archeologist Marija Gimbutas wrote in her book *The Goddesses and Gods of Old Europe*: *"The role of the deer in Old European Myth was not a creation of Neolithic agriculturists. The importance of a pregnant doe must have been inherited from a pre-agricultural era...In some portrayals, deer antlers and crescent moons merge together as they spin around a cross with knobbed extremities showing the four cardinal points of the world. Two pairs of opposed crescents and the goddess' dog can also be seen."* [53] Again, we see the lunar connections, the Goddess and her dog (which is a wolf).

In the Strasbourg Museum of Archaeology, there is an icon of a god which shows the connection between the Old Religion and the stag and the wolf. It was discovered at Mout Donon, near a Celtic shrine to Mercury. Here is depicted a woodland god carrying the first fruits of the forest, including a pinecone, acorns,

---

53   Marija Gimbutas, *The Goddesses and Gods of Old Europe* (University of California Press, 2007) 94.

and nuts, in an open bag underneath his left arm. He is shown wearing a wolf-skin and carrying a long hunting knife, which hangs on his left side. His boots are decorated with a small animal head appearing at the top of each boot. The god's paradoxical role as a hunter and protector is shown by the wolf-skin cloak and weapons he bears, and by the stag he gently rests his hands upon. It is in this icon that we see the connection between the God of the Old Religion and the images of the stag and the wolf. He is shown as both the hunter and protector of all forest animals. He is the Guardian of the Grove, the Lord of the Trees, the Old One.

The image of the stag and the wolf also appears in icons of the Celtic god known as Cernunnos. The famous Gundestrup cauldron depicts Cernunnos with a wolf on his left, and a Stag to his right. This seems to be a common theme in many different parts of Europe, and I believe there is a good chance that they share a common source.

In an early Roman mosaic, an interesting image captures the transition from hunter-gatherer societies to an agricultural community. In the book *Roman Life* by Mary Johnston, a mosaic is shown divided into three sections, displaying the evolution of ancient Italic society. The bottom portion shows a human hunter wearing a cloak made of stag's skin, with a stag's head upon his own. He is pictured sneaking up on his prey and herding them into a prepared trap. Above this scene is a crude encampment where people are tilling the soil and employing various animals for labor. In the upper top portion, we find a classical Roman structure, depicting people in classical attire with domesticated animals. A stag and a wolf are also shown fleeing the more modern part of the human community. Captured here in this mosaic is the story of our ancestors and the story of the stag and the wolf,

The Stag & The Wolf

who were gradually driven out of communities. It is interesting to note, in this same book, a picture of a Lares shrine depicting two Lares holding drinking vessels adorned with a stag head. Lares were originally deities of cultivated fields and later represented the spirits of Roman ancestors. In some agricultural societies, the presence of deer or stag posed a threat to the crops, so it's unlikely they would—at least on the surface—revere these creatures. So, why would the ancients have depicted the Lares holding drinking cups with a stag head? The answer is contained within the imagery itself. A drinking cup contains the essence which it receives and serves to pass this essence on to whoever drinks from it. The stag cups represent the original connection with the God of the Forest, who later became the Slain God of the Harvest. It is a remembrance of where the "essence" of the Old Religion had come from in the first place.

As stated earlier, the goddess Diana is often depicted in art accompanied by either a stag or a hound. In some art forms, we also find her with the god Pan. Again, we see the domesticated version of her earlier consort, the Stag God. In a Greek legend associated with Diana, Actaeon comes upon Artemis (the Greek Diana) in the woods bathing, and stops to admire her beauty. One of her followers takes notice of him, and angered that a mere mortal has seen her nude, Artemis turns him into a stag. His hunting dogs then turn on him, tearing him apart.

In another mythos, Diana and an older Actaeon are closely related to the Mystery Tradition of the Old Religion. In this myth, Diana falls in love with the god Actaeon, but because of her reputation as a chaste goddess, she grieves for a love she feels she can never experience. An adversary of Actaeon discovers Diana's secret and plots against Actaeon. Disguised as a friend, the adversary approaches Diana and bids her to change Actaeon into a stag when he enters the forest, claiming that in this form, she could proclaim her love for him without drawing any attention. Diana agrees and sets out to seduce Actaeon. Knowing his usual hunting places, Diana decides to bathe nude in a stream, so that Actaeon will come across her. When Actaeon does see Diana, she transforms him into a stag and leaves her bath to go to him. They become lovers, and Actaeon remains in the forest as a stag god. Unfortunately, one day, as Actaeon was intending to surprise Diana during her bath, a pack of wolves comes across him and he flees. He is overrun and perishes, having been brought down by the leader of the wolf pack (which is what his adversary had planned all along).

In *The Goddesses and Gods of Old Europe*, Dr. Marija Gimbutas writes: *"The Lady of free and untamed nature and the Mother, protectress of weaklings, a divinity in whom the contrasting principles of virginity and motherhood are fused into the concept of a single goddess, was venerated in Groece, Lydia, Crete and Italy. She appears as Artemis and under many local names: Diktynna, Pasiphae, Europa ("the wide-glancing one"), Britomartis ("the sweet virgin") in Crete, Laphria in Actolia, Kallisto ("the beautiful) in Arkadia, or Agrotera ("the wild"), and Diana in Rome... The stag is her standing attribute in plastic art; she is called "stag-huntress" in the Homeric Hymns."* [54]

In her conclusions, Dr. Gimbutas writes: *"The teaching of Western Civilization starts with the Greeks and rarely do people ask themselves what forces lay behind these beginnings. But European civilization was not created in the space of a few centuries; the roots are deeper—by six thousand years. That is to say, vestiges of the myths and*

---

54 Marija Gimbutas, *The Goddesses and Gods of Old Europe* (University of California Press, 2007) 198.

artistic concepts of Old Europe, which endured from the seventh to the fourth millennium BC were transmitted to the modern Western world and became part of its cultural heritage." [55]

When we research the mythos of the stag and wolf, we find a widespread legend, connecting people from Italy, up into France, and through the British Isles. It seems quite reasonable to conclude that there was a common origin to this concept, and that we can all trace our traditions back to one common belief system. An altar set with stag horns awakens a common spiritual mentality across devotees of the Stag God. It is there in our very being; it is part of us. The wolf too speaks to us, and the memory of its place in our Mysteries is now hidden in the occult associations of werewolves. The werewolf legend, though altered by Christian revisions (as is common with most Pagan images), still contains elements of the Wolf Cult, which once was a part of the Old Religion. Those were the early warrior cults in which the men first came to understand their own Mysteries. They were fearful and dangerous, but controlled by the matriarchal priestesses before the male cults rose to power.

Interestingly, only a silver sword or bullet slays a werewolf (silver being a lunar symbol), the Full Moon transforms them into one, and a pentagram appears on their bodies! All these ancient symbols are still associated with Witchcraft and are ingrained in the human psyche. These ancient memories call to us, beckon us, and awaken us to the Old Ways.

---

55 Marija Gimbutas, *The Goddesses and Gods of Old Europe* (University of California Press, 2007) 238.

Mama Strega's Spellbook

Psychic Self-Defense

When you must protect yourself from a psychic or magickal attack, it is essential that you protect your home and your person. To secure your home, it is advisable to establish at least three levels of defense.

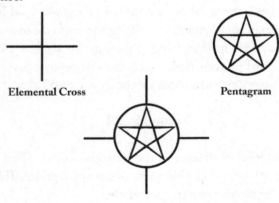

Elemental Cross

Pentagram

First Level

The first level of defense involves placing seals on each doorway and window of your home. The most important room is your bedroom, because most attacks will occur while you sleep. It is normally effective to trace (with fingers or a ritual tool) a protective symbol upon each glass window. The Elemental Cross, together with a pentagram, is especially effective. These seals may be visualized or physically marked out.

Each symbol must be traced three times while visualizing a glowing white light. After tracing the sign, point directly at its center, and say:

> *"I place thee here*
> *in the name of the Source of All Things,*
> *that to this place,*
> *no evil thing approach,*
> *or enter in!"*

Next, cense the window or door with dragon's blood incense. During times of actual attack, you will have to re-do the seals nightly.

You may wish to place hand mirrors in the window and upon the headboard of your bed, especially during attacks. Placing images of your deities in these locations will also help.

Second Level

The second level of defense is the "charged object." This can be an amulet, statue, or anything you deem appropriate. This level also includes the use of a magick circle.

There are many techniques for charging an object. Usually, you would employ an Elemental charge, along with a pentagram charge. It is especially effective to hang a charged crystal in each window, and another one over your bed. For extra protection, place a few large natural crystals around your bedroom and any room where you entertain guests.

The Pentagram Charge
Set a small metal dish on your worktable, along with the object to be charged. Pour some Strega Liquore into the bowl, about two-thirds full. Ignite the liquid with a match, saying:

"I bless thee in the name of the Source of All Things."

Visualize a blue five-pointed star rising out of the flames. Then, mentally transfer it to the object you wish to charge. Visualize the object glowing blue as a star enters it. At this point, you will point at the glowing object and say:

"I bless thee in the name of the Source of All Things,
I give thee charge and strict watch,
That in thy presence, no evil thing approach,
Or enter in!"

During attack, you should cast a magick circle around your bed before going to sleep. Wearing of a protective pentagram or any amulet is wise and effective too. A quartz stone is an effective choice.

Third Level

The third level of defense employs guardians and counterattacks. The guardians can be various spirits, thought-forms, familiars, or other entities. Counterattack can include the use of ritual tools to fend off an attack, performing of a ritual, or sensing energy spheres.

Before sleep, visualize a bird of prey perched nearby. Form an energy sphere between your palms and charge it with a command to protect you from any intrusion (astral entities, for example). Next, send this sphere to the bird, and give it a verbal or mental command to protect and defend.

If the psychic attack is serious, keep your spirit blade nearby (pointing at you). Also, don't underestimate the effectiveness of turning on a bright light when you sense danger! The light will disperse any astral form in the area.

Select Articles from Moon Shadow

This section is a collection of articles which first appeared in the Moon Shadow magazine, which was renamed Raven's Call in the Fall of 1992.

We have assembled a collection of articles which reflect the Italian Witch Culture and hope that you will find them of interest.

Walnut Witches

In Northern Europe, legends abound of great gatherings of Witches on Brocken Mountain. In Italy, the Witches convened at an old walnut tree in Benevento.

Manuscripts from old Witch trials speak of this Walnut Tree, which was said to had always been there in leaf all year long. The tree's nuts were described as pyramid-like in form, and many were sold as talismans or amulets. The tree's large size, with thick branches full of leaves, was renowned for its ability to provide shade that was as dark as night itself.

When I was a child, my mother told me stories of the Witches in Benevento and the walnut tree. She grew up in Naples, which is about fifty miles west of Benevento, and she was often herself called "Strega di Benevento" (the Witch of Benevento). According to my mother, the Witches of the area would assemble at the tree in Benevento and sing and dance through the night. At some point, groups of Witches would leave the gathering and hold their own private rites in some secret place. One of the songs which she remembers does indeed speak of going off into the night, away from the walnut tree.

The walnut Witches were said to have been a powerful group, actively psychic, and dedicated to the Old Religion. Through their tireless efforts, the Craft survived intact and was never driven totally "underground" in Benevento.

In 662 CE, a man named Romuald became the Duke of Benevento. He was Pagan and was known to have joined in the celebrations around the tree. At the same time, there was a man named Barbato, who would later become a Christian bishop and saint. Hard times befell Benevento, and the army of the Byzantine Emperor Constans II threatened to invade.

Barbato blamed the Witches and their religion. With the threat of invasion looming, the people of Benevento renounced the local practices. Barbato had the tree cut down and converted Romuald to Christianity (at least in name). Barbato was said to have built a church upon the spot where the tree had stood, but another tree seeded grew again in the same spot.

Whatever the case may be, my mother tells me that a Witch's walnut tree now stands in the Stretto di Barba, near the river. Witches still gather there today in secret, although the town is not unsympathetic.

The Witches of Benevento were never, at least in early Christian times, labeled devil worshipers. Their "crime" was heresy, for they were known as worshipers of Diana. It was not until much later that the Church called them devil worshipers, which was never true of their religion.

The walnut Witches of Benevento were very well known for their healing and for dispensing coins to the poor. In Charles Leland's book *Etruscan Magic and Occult Remedies*, there are several exaggerated stories concerning the good Witches of Benevento and their service to the community. Fortunately, the good reputation of Benevento's Witches has outweighed centuries of Christian slander, and the Old Religion is alive and well in Benevento.

The Triad Traditions

In fourteenth-century Italy, a wise woman called Aradia brought about the reorganization of the Old Religion, also known as *La Vecchia Religione*. From her efforts, three traditions arose out of one. These Traditions are now known as the Fanarra, Janarra, and Tanarra.

The Fanarra are centered in Northern Italy and are known as the Keepers of the Earth Mysteries. The Janarra and Tanarra occupy central Italy. The Janarra are the Keepers of the Lunar Mysteries, and the Tanarra are the Keepers of the Stellar Wall Mysteries.

The leader of each Tradition is called a *Grimas*, and each Grimas has a working knowledge of the other two Mystery Traditions. Initiates are trained in the ways of each Tradition (respectively), and, if they choose to be priests and priestesses, they can begin training in the mystery teachings of the other two Traditions.

The Aridian Tradition in the United States blends the Triad Traditions to restore the original Tradition that Aradia returned to the people.

The Fanarric Teachings reveal the mysteries of what are commonly referred to as ley lines. They also reveal the secrets of the earth's power and the use of places (and objects) for directing energy. Janarric Teachings reveal the mysteries of lunar energy and their use in magick and Nature. Tanarric Teachings reveal the secrets of ancient stellar cults, star lore, and the nature of stellar forces.

Common to all three systems are the arts of herbalism, divination, magick, ritual, and other aspects associated with the Old Religion. Each Tradition enhances these arts with their own individual mystery teachings.

During the latter part of the fourteenth century, the original tradition divided into three separate traditions to safeguard the Mystery Teachings during the era of persecution by the Christian Church. Today, these old traditions are fading in the Old Country. Yet, isolated covens in remote mountain villages still hold to the Old Ways. Seaport cities like Naples still hold small Janarric covens, and Benevento, once the capital of La Vecchia Religione, provides sanctuary for only a few hereditary covens. The seed of that old walnut tree has been planted in modern times, and with the aid of the Goddess, a new age of the Old Religion has begun.

Witchcraft in Tuscany

In Northern Italy lies the region of Toscana, or Tuscany. In this area dwell the descendants of an ancient people known as the Etruscans. It is here that the Old Religion of Italy has been preserved by Witches who have passed down their Craft through unbroken lines for countless generations.

In the United States, the Craft Tradition is quite unique, even by Italian standards. In it, we see the remnants of early Etruscan religious belief. The mythos of Tuscan Witchcraft are largely those of spirits who were once Etruscan gods.

The magick of Tuscany is one of folk magick and bears little resemblance to modern ceremonial practices. To Tuscan Witches, their Craft is a legacy that must be passed to at least one other person before they die. If they do not, it is said to interfere with the proper advancement of future lives. In the Tuscan system, a Witch is reborn as a human many times, becoming more powerful. Eventually, the individual becomes a spirit, and may possibly even become a god.

The magickal focus is largely upon spells, omens, and natural objects. This also included amulets, talismans, charm bags, and divination. Natural actions, such as a "falling star" or fruit dropping from a branch, may be employed in spells. For example, an incan-

Raven's Call

tation might be recited to connect the falling action to a wish that someone may "fall" in love, or perhaps that an enemy might "fall."

Ritual circles are rarely employed for spell casting or other magickal practices. A large, flat rock situated within a field would suffice for any Tuscan Witch. Symbols could be arranged in patterns around power objects placed upon the flat rock, and the Witch's wand (the primary tool of Tuscan Witches) would be passed over them, executing ritual gestures. Metered tonal chants are always employed in every act of magick, which is one of the most cherished arts of Tuscan Witchcraft.

The central deities in Tuscany are the god Tinia and the goddess Uni. They rule the Universe, which is comprised of sixteen "houses," four in each quarter. The gods of destiny dwell in the North; in the East, the major gods; in the South, astral entities; and in the West, the beings of the Underworld. Tinia and Uni rule over a hierarchy of powerful spirits, which exert power and influence over the Earth.

The following list will show the relationship between the gods and the spirits of Tuscany:

Tuscan	Greek/Roman
Teramo	Mercury
Nortia	Fortuna
Aplu	Apollo
Losna	Diana/Luna
Turanna	Venus
Pano	Pan
Maso	Mars

Witchcraft in Tuscany

Tuscan	Greek/Roman
Silviano	Silvanus
Esta	Vesta
Sentiero	Terminus
Faflon	Bacchus
Tesana	Aurora
Spulviero	Aeolus
Fanio	Faunus
Alpena	Flora
Tituno	Vulcan
Verbio	Verbius
Dusio	Eros
Jano	Janus
Meana	Fata

These spirits are evoked for many purposes and are more part of everyday life in Tuscany compared to other Craft regions. The lore of Tuscany is so pervasive that even the average Christian is familiar.

Teramo is a messenger spirit evoked to carry requests to the gods, and to aid in manifesting magickal success. Losna is the spirit of the Moon evoked to aid in all works of magick. Turanna has influence over matters of love. In the Old Religion of Tuscany, everything is a result of either a spirit or god's action, or that of a Witch. This is one reason why everyday life is so closely tied to the Old Ways.

As in most Craft Traditions, the basic Elemental Forces are revered, and living entities are associated with the seemingly magickal properties of the Elements. Likewise, Nature is seen to be filled with spirits, which inhabit objects and places.

Fauni and *silvani* are spirits of the woods, and *falletti* are wind spirits. *Monachetti* are gnome-like spirits, and *linchetti* are elf-like spirits.

In Tuscan Witchcraft, the North quarter is a place of great power. The Elemental beings of the North are called *palas* (originally the palas shared the southern sphere of influence with those entities known as *settiano*). They are very etheric and have influence over mental processes, creativity, thought, concepts, and so on. In the South are the *settrano*, who are spirits of Elemental Fire. They have power over activity, motivation, vitality, and the like. In the West are the *lasa* who are spirits of Elemental Water. They have influence over inner motivation, the subconscious, life fluids, and so on. In early lore, the *lasa* were also spirits associated with the Underworld. Through the interaction of these beings, vegetation flourishes, rains fall, and life cycles continue. These spirits are the inner forces of Nature.

Closely linked to the belief in these spirits is a large tradition of magickal cures, incantations, spells, and rites for attracting love, banishing evil, and assuring physical comforts. All of these have been passed down through family lines, where the belief that Witches are born again through their descendants is prevalent. Even though much of the lore is known to non-Witches, the secrets of the practical art are closely guarded by hereditary Witch Clans.

Witchcraft in Tuscany

It was in the region of Old Tuscany that Aradia, the Holy Strega, was born. Aradia was taught the Old Religion from an early age by her aunt, growing up in the consciousness of a different world. Hers was a world steeped in the witch lore of Tuscany, a world which allowed her the freedom to explore the inner and outer realities.

Assured of her future and having found favor with the God and Goddess, Aradia formed covens in the Alban Hills region near the ancient Lake of Nemi. It was here that Aradia blended her own spiritual understanding with the Old Ways, and brought about a revival of the Old Religion, which embraced peasant and noble alike.

The Watchers:
Secrets of the Tanarric Witches

As early as 3000 BCE, the early stellar cults believed in four "royal" stars (known as Lords) called the Watchers. Each one of these stars "ruled" over one of the four cardinal points.

The star Aldebaran, when it marked the spring equinox, held the position of Watcher of the East. Regulus, marking the summer solstice, was Watcher of the South. Antares, marking the autumn equinox, was Watcher of the West. Fomalhaut, marking the winter solstice, was Watcher of the North. Towers were constructed, bearing the symbols of the Watchers, for the worship of these Watchers, and their symbols were set upon these towers for the purpose of evocation. During the "Rites of Calling," the stars were traced in the air with a ritual wand, and the secret names of the Watchers were called out.

In the Stellar Mythos, the Watchers themselves were gods who guarded the Heavens and the Earth. Their nature and rank were altered by the successive lunar and solar cults, which replaced the stellar cults. Eventually, the Greeks reduced them to gods of the four winds, and the Christians reduced them to principalities of the air. Their connection with the stars is vaguely recalled in the Christian concept of heavenly angels.

Cabalists organized them into archangels, which may derive from the early Hebrew concept of angels known as the Watchers. According to this belief, the Watchers were ruled over by four greater Watchers known as Michael, Gabriel, Raphael, and Auriel.

In the Italian Witch Cult, these ancient beings are the *Grigori*. They are the Guardians of the Planes, protectors of the ritual circle, and witnesses to what has been passed through the ages. Each of the Grigori ruled over a Watchtower, which acted as a portal marking the four quarters of a ritual circle. In ancient times, the Watchtowers were similar to a military fighting unit, except they defended the home.

In Italian Witch lore, the stars were once thought of as the campfires of Watcher legions. Originally, the Watchers were "lesser gods" who watched over the Earth and the Heavens. In the Aridian Mythos, they were the guardians of the four entrances to the Realm of Aster, which is the home of the Gods. Outside of the Craft, the Watchers are commonly linked to the concept of "guardian angels." In the Hebrew Bible, there is reference made to the *Iryin,* or Watchers, which appear to be an order of angels. In the apocryphal books of Enoch and Jubilees, the Watchers are mentioned as fallen angels originally sent to Earth to teach humans law and justice. In the Book of Enoch, the Watchers (called therein Grigori) are listed as rebellious angels who followed Satanael in a heavenly war.

In Rabbinic and Cabalistic lore, the "good" Watchers dwell in the fifth heaven, and the "evil" Watchers dwell in the third heaven. The Watchers of the fifth heaven are ruled over by the archangels Uriel, Raphael, Michael, and Gabriel. In the *Apocryphon of Genesis,* it is said that Noah is the offspring of a Watcher who slept with Bat-Enosh, his mother.

In *A Dictionary of Angels*, the Watchers are also listed as the fallen angels who instructed men in the arts.

- **Armaros** taught the resolving of enchantments
- **Araqiel** taught the signs of the earth
- **Azazel** taught the art of cosmetics
- **Barqel** taught astrology
- **Armaros** taught the resolving of enchantments
- **Araqiel** taught the signs of the earth
- **Azazel** taught the art of cosmetics
- **Barqel** taught astrology
- **Ezequiel** taught the knowledge of the clouds
- **Gadreel** taught the making of weapons of war
- **Kokabiel** taught the mystery of the Stars
- **Renemue** taught writing
- **Sariel** taught the knowledge of the Moon
- **Samyaza** taught herbal enchantments
- **Shamsiel** taught the signs of the Sun

It is these same angels who are referred to as the Sons of God in the Book of Genesis. Their "sins" filled the Earth with violence, and the world was destroyed because of their intervention. This, of course, is the biblical account, and has little to do with Craft concepts.

Richard Cavendish, in his book *The Powers of Evil*, makes references to the possibilities of the giants mentioned in Genesis 6:4. He also lists the Watchers as the fallen angels that magicians call forth in ceremonial magick.

Despite misinformation in Cavendish's books, he does draw parallels and even mentions that the Watchers were named such because they were stars, the "eyes of night."

St. Paul, in the New Testament, calls the fallen angels principalities: *"For we are not contending against flesh and blood, but against the principalities, against the powers. against the spiritual hosts of wickedness in High Places..."* [56]

It was also St. Paul who referred to Satan as "the prince of power of the air," thereby establishing the connection between Satan (who is associated with "a star" in Isaiah 14:12) and etheric beings, which later came to be known as demons and principalities of the air. This theme was later developed by a sixteenth-century French theologian named Sinistrari, who spoke of beings existing between humans and angels. He called them demons and associated them with the Elemental natures of Earth, Air, Fire, and Water.

Cardinal Newman, writing in the mid-1800s, proposed that certain angels existed who were neither totally good nor evil, but had only "partially fallen" from the Heavens. This would seem to support placing the Watchers in two different Heavens. These are examples of how a central theme can be divided and transformed. Today, even among some Craft Traditions, there exists a great deal of confusion concerning the Watchers.

I receive a large amount of mail from initiates of all levels and traditions, seeking clarification on this topic. Some systems view them as Elemental rulers, demi-gods, guardians, spiritual teachers, planetary intelligences, and even angels. All these concepts are, indeed, aspects of the Watchers.

To understand the Watchers, we need only look to their role in some Witchcraft traditions. Our first encounter with these entities usually occurs when casting a ritual circle. The Watchers are called, or evoked, to guard the circle and to witness the ritual.

---

56 *King James Bible*, Eph. 6:12

Their roles as guardians of a ceremonial circle are self-explanatory, but why are they witnesses?

Let us consider the relationship that exists between a Witch and the Watchers. When a seeker is initiated, they are brought before the quarters. The initiate is then presented before the Watcher of the quarter, and the initiate's Craft name is revealed. From that moment on, the initiate is "watched" and aided by the Watchers. A bond builds that serves as a safeguard for every act of magick that a Witch performs.

The Watchers guard the portals to the astral realms, and they allow or dispel a magickal act in astrally. This is why certain gestures and signs of evocation, such as the pentagram (there's that star again!), were designed to announce a trained practitioner (one who had sworn not to misuse the Arts). There is a definite link between the powers of a Witch and the rapport with the Watchers.

In the lore of the Witch Cult, the Watchers assist in the spiritual growth of a Witch and escort them to the next realm after physical death. Nothing is ever hidden from the Watchers, and, in the end, a Witch may come to know them as the "Dread Lords of the Outer Spaces," or the "Mighty Ones." This isn't a scenario where they will "get you" if you're not "good," but rather an assurance that karma will be delivered promptly.

As we have seen already, the Watchers were linked to certain stars that marked the solstices and equinoxes, the cornerstones of the year. On a greater scale, the Watchers oversaw the seasons of the Heavens as well. It is important to remember that the Watchers are stellar beings, not lunar. Their association with a lunar cult, rather than a solar, is obvious on a mundane scale. Stars are associated with the night, as is the Moon, for they share the heavens together. The Sun is seemingly alone (at least most of the time). The stellar and lunar cults predate the solar cults, which later assimilated and adapted the inner teachings of the preceding cults.

In ancient lore, the Watchers once had bodies of matter but evolved beyond the need for them long before the rise of humankind. They became beings of light, which is likely one of the first parallels between Watchers and angels. Yet, these beings were linked to the stars even before their evolution, for the old legends say that the Watchers came from the stars. In the early stellar cults, the association was so strong that the Watchers were considered the stars themselves who had descended to Earth.

From their original worship as gods, the Watchers are honored as spiritual beings overseeing the worlds. In between, we have seen what became of them. Today, we acknowledge them as guardians of the entrances and exits to and from the worlds that connect to the physical plane. We also know them as the "Keepers of the Ancient Wisdom" and "Guardians of the Art."

Herbs of the Old Religion

Of all the herbs associated with the Old Religion, rue and fennel deserve special mention. Let us examine each herb, its properties, and its associations with the ancient Craft.

Rue (Ruta graveolens)

Rue is native to Italy and Southern Europe. It is a hardy evergreen perennial, growing approximately up to three feet tall. Rue contains a powerful stimulant known as rutin. Herbalists have long employed rue as a stimulant and antispasmodic. Ancient writings attribute the curing of many illnesses to rue, as well as the restoration of good eyesight. Hippocrates considered it an essential ingredient in antidotes to poison.

Along with its many physical attributes, this herb also has a rich magickal and religious history. An Italian Witch charm, called the *cimaruta* (sprig of rue), bore the symbol of a rue branch, hung with symbols. During the Middles Ages, rue was associated with Witches, both as a ward against them and as their main herb. Ironically, the Catholic Church used its branch to sprinkle holy water on its followers and named it an "herb of grace."

Raven's Call

Rue is used in several rituals where it represents the God and his power. The mythos of the God, as reflected in planting, growing, and harvesting, is played out through the use of rue in a series of seasonal rites. Various parts of the plant are employed as they relate to the symbology of the God. The following are a few of the traditional associations connected to rue.

Ruler: Sun
God Form: Faunus
Goddess Form: Fana
Medicinal: Healing
Magickal: Protection
Ritual: A God-form plant

Fennel (Foeniculum vulgare)

An herb indigenous to the shores of the Mediterranean, fennel was well known among the ancients, and was cultivated by the Romans for its aromatic fruits and succulent edible shoots. It also had a reputation for strengthening eyesight. In medieval times, it was hung over doors on Midsummer Eve to ward off evil spirits.

Fennel has a thick root stock growing to five feet or more in height. Roman fennel is distinguished by its greater length and stronger anise-like fragrance. Florence fennel is smaller, growing only a few feet in height, and more bushy in appearance.

In the Midsummer Festivals of Adonis, fennel was among those seeds planted in pots for the rituals, which represented his death and resurrection. The seeds sprouted quickly, and the sprouts were then allowed to wither from the Sun and drought.

Herbs of the Old Religion

During the sixteenth and seventeenth century, Italian Witch trials revealed a curious tradition associated with fennel. Certain Witches, calling themselves Benandanti, gave accounts of ritual battles (performed in "dream states"), which occurred four times a year. These battles were waged against an evil cult (the Malandanti) over the harvest yields. The Benandanti fought with long stalks of fennel, and the Malandanti with sorghum stalks. At these battles, the Benandanti carried a standard bearing a banner of white silk with a gilded lion upon it. The Malandanti carried a banner of red silk with four black devils.

In Italian Craft rituals today, fennel is used as a symbol of victory and is presented at each of the Elemental quarters during the spring equinox and the summer solstice. At these times, it represents a successful harvest empowered by the magick of the coven. Here are a few traditional associations of fennel.

Ruler: Mars
God Form: Dianus
Goddess Form: Diana
Medicinal: Stomach problems
Magickal: Protection
Ritual: Victory, success, dominion

The Gesture of Power

The Gesture of Power can be used as a tool for evocation and charging objects. It can also be used to open and close a ritual circle. Before performing the gesture, read through these instructions carefully, so that you understand this technique completely.

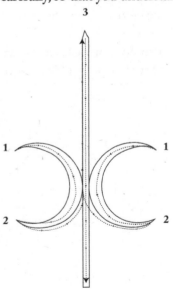

Hold the wand in your left hand, and the dagger in your right. Extend both arms out to your sides. Then, bring both tools inward to the first position. Next, move the tools down in a circular manner to the second position. Each tool will be tracing a separate crescent. Bring both together crossed up to the third position. Finally, while concentrating, bring the tools down to fourth position, imagining that you are drawing down power. The fourth position must bring the tools into contact with the object being charged or the area to which the evocation is directed.

To cut a cast circle, go to your point of exit and cross the wand and blade, assuming the third position. Move them down to the fourth position, then the second, which will uncross the tools.

Move to the first position in a circular motion, and then stretch the arms out. This will unseal your circle.

To close the opening, simply perform the original procedure in entirety where the opening was created.

Each time you perform the gesture, you will trace the symbol as pictured. Look at the symbol and practice following the outline. Do not move outside of the image as you pass through the positions. With practice, you will find this technique quite useful. You may wish to enhance this technique by visualizing the symbol glowing as you trace it in the air.

For charging, you may wish to mentally condense the image into a glowing sphere, and then transfer it into the objects with your tools.

The Cimaruta

In the Bologna Museum, there is a small Etruscan amulet called the *cimaruta*. As late as the mid-eighteenth century, the cimaruta was a common charm against the evil eye. In Naples, it was often worn upon the breasts of infants for protection. The cimaruta is a sprig of rue, which is the Neapolitan name for rue, *cima di ruta*. It is divided into three main branches, which can represent Diana Triformis, composed of Hecate, Diana, and Proserpine. On the tips of the branches hung six symbolic charms:

Hand: Magick
Fish: Phallic/Fertility
Serpent or Crescent: Guardianship
Key: Access to power (opening of Portals)
Blade: A five-petaled flower blossom, symbolizing protection

Before it became popular, it was used by Witches as a sign of membership in the Witch Cult. As time passed, it began to be called the Witch charm. Doreen Valiente, in her book *An ABC of Witchcraft,* says it was used as a sign that someone was a devotee of Diana, the Queen of the Witches.

The Spirits of Italy

The Folletto

There are many different types of spirits in Italian folklore. One of the most common and widely known is the *folletto*, or *folletti* in its plural form. Folletti travel in the wind and can be seen at play, causing swirls in the dust (or "knots of winds" in Italian). They are said to be like butterflies, always moving about. Traditionally, the folletto is friendly towards humans, but can be mischievous and annoying at times. It is not uncommon for the folletto to conjure wind and lift a dress or knock over objects with a sudden gust. They are magickal beings, and have a particular attraction to sexual situations.

In Stregheria, a folletto can be called the *basadone* (woman-kisser) in northern Italy and are known to steal kisses from women with a passing breeze.

Another type of folletto is a spirit called the *linchetto* (plural *linchetti)*. Unlike the air sprite folletto, the linchetto work mostly at night. Linchetti are native to the Tuscan region of Italy, which was the seat of Etruria. These spirits are said to cause nightmares and noises in the night. Linchetti are said to hate disorder and will not dwell in any messy spaces.

Raven's Call

One old technique to drive away the linchetto was to spill seeds upon the floor around your bed. The night spirit would come and try to pick up the seeds, usually leaving in frustration. Another technique was to place a lock of curly hair over the bed. The linchetto would try all night to straighten it, then flee in despair.

The Laúru and Fata

The *fata* (*fate* plural) is a spirit of the woods and water. They are beautiful, gentle, and kind. The fate are excellent shapeshifters, often appearing as old people. Sometimes, they will change into young women or various small animals. In legend, the fate would disguise themselves as old women or animals, asking for help. Those who helped them were richly rewarded, but anyone who was cruel risked their health and fortune.

The *laúru* is a folletto spirit with black twinkling eyes, long curly hair, and clothes of fine velvet. They tend to be mischievous and enjoy teasing human children. When treated with respect, the laúru may reveal hidden treasures, or supply the winning lottery numbers. Like most Italian spirits, the males love human women and seek to seduce them in dreams. According to folklore, a pair of ram or bull horns hung over a doorway keep the laúru away.

The Massariol, Fauni, and the Silvani

In Italy, there are three specific spirits with similar qualities: the *massariol,* the *fauni,* and the *silvani*. The massariol are known as the "Little Farmers." They are about a foot high and dress in red costume, wearing a large hat. Massariol usually spend their time in gardens and barnyards, caring for plants and animals. The

The Spirits of Italy

male elves have a certain fancy for human women and sometimes change into grooming articles to be close to their bodies. The massariol have a cheerful disposition and are helpful to humans.

The fauni and silvani are known as the "Goat People." The fauni are field spirits that have power over animals. The silvani guard herd animals, as well as house and land boundaries. These spirits appear pan-like with large genitals. Both spirits prefer light airy woods and fields, and can best be seen when breezes move through vegetation. They are not unfriendly to humans (unless they abuse animals,) but are known to be somewhat mischievous.

The Lares

In the Old Religion of Italy, the *Lares* are both protectors and preservers. In Roman mythology, they were ancestral spirits and guarded the family. Upon the house's hearth, a small Lares house was placed. Each Lares house had a receptacle for offerings, which consisted of wine, honey, milk and flowers.

The focal point of a family is their home, and in ancient times, the focal point of a house was the hearth. A prayer was said to the Lares every morning, and special offerings were made at family festivals. These spirits may have previously been gods of the cultivated fields, worshipped by each household at the crossroads, where its allotment joined those of others. Later, they were worshipped in houses, and the household Lares were the center of the family cult. A was usually a youthful figure, dressed in a short tunic, holding a drinking horn in one hand, and a cup in the other.

In early Etruscan times, these spirits were called the *lasa*. In Tuscany, the name lasa still applies to various spirits.

Aradia, who according to some traditions lived in Tuscany during the fourteenth century, taught about the lasa and their relationship to fire. The flame became a symbol of the Spirit of the Old Religion. Aradia associated the light of fire with personal enlightenment. She taught that we all bear a spark or flame of divine consciousness within us. This was our spirit or soul.

Fire is an ancient symbol of deity and of worship. To early humankind, it provided warmth and protection, as well as a method of food preparation. The possession of fire was essential to long term survival. Today, it appears on the Aridian altar as the Spirit Flame, which represents the presence of deity.

In La Vecchia Religione, the Lares represent not only ancient family ties, but the spirits who protect and preserve the Old Religion. Because the Lares Cult maintains a strong family connection, hereditary Witches of Italy still exist today. Generations have remembered and honored the previous generations, passing on the ancient traditions of the Old Religion. Even today, elements of the ancient cult still exist. The tradition of the Witch Befana, for example, is believed by some to be a living remnant of the Old Religion. It is interesting to note that children write their wishes upon bits of paper, which are then placed in the hearth to be carried up the chimney (connecting fire, the Lares, and the Befana).

La Befana

As previously told, the Legend of Befana is still a living myth in Italy today. On the Epiphany, children set out stockings to be filled with presents by the good Witch, La Befana—a curious tradition to have survived in a Catholic Christian nation! Curious, unless you realize that the Old Religion never totally disappeared in Italy.

The Spirits of Italy

In her book, *Celebrating Italy,* Carol Field tells of Befana and her ancient association to Hecate. Here, she writes: *"The good and bad sides of the Befana are like the good mother/bad witch of fairy tales, two aspects of a single person. The Befana may bring wonderful presents, but she can also be a grotesque woman with a sinister black face, associated in some accounts with Hecate, Queen of the Night."*[57]

La Befana by Bartolomeo Pinelli (1821)

Field shares an etching done by Bartolomeo Pinelli in 1825, in which Befana is seated, surrounded by an abundance of fruits, grains, and other harvest items. In her hand, she holds a stalk of

---

57 Carol Fields, *Celebrating Italy: The Tastes and Traditions of Italy Through Its Feasts, Festivals & Sumptuous Foods* (HarperCollins, 1997).

fennel, upon which a stocking is suspended. Here, she may represent the Great Mother amidst the fruits of the Earth.

The author recounts a time she observed the burning of an effigy of Befana during a New Year celebration. A procession began at sunset, wandering through the village and up to a site upon a hill. This parade, she states, is always led by the oldest man in the community. Upon the hill was a pyramid-style stock of corn sheaves, brushwood, and pine branches. Upon the top of these stacks, an effigy of Befana is placed. The stack is set on fire by the men of the village, led by the oldest. Chestnuts are roasted on the fire as symbols of fertility. It is said that, if the smoke blows to the East, it portends a year of abundance. If it blows to the West, then the crops will be poor. Once the fire had died, the embers were removed and scattered over the fields, which will later be planted. This echoes the sacrificial king mythos of the Slain God.

There are two books that associate the Befana with certain seasonal rites and reveal her connection to the Goddess in ancient times. The first is written by Franco Cardini, called *The Sacred Day: A Book of Festivals*. This book focuses on festivals and their connections with myth, rituals, and magickal rites. The other is *The Calendar: Festivals, Myths, Legends, and Rites of the Year* by Alberto Cattabiani. Field draws upon these research texts throughout her book. A wealth of information can be found in these books, supporting the survival of pre-Christian Cults into modern times. For example, the Befana may have originally been Diana. Italian Witches maintained the presence of the Goddess Diana throughout the ages, which Leland documented in his work *Aradia*.

Julio Caro Baroja, in his book *The World of Witches*, writes: *"There seems to have been a flourishing cult of Diana among European country people in the 5th and 6th centuries, and she was generally looked upon as*

The Spirits of Italy

the woods and fields, except by those trying to root out the cult, who thought she was a devil. Occasionally, she appeared in the company of certain Spirits referred to as dianae—according to texts such as that of St. Martin of Braga which deal with beliefs of country-folk in the north-western regions of the Iberian Peninsula."[58]

He adds that the Cult of Diana also worshiped a male "Dianum." Century after century, this is a common theme in Italian Witch trials. Are we seeing Befana with a consort before they were dethroned by the Christian Church?

---

58 Julio Baroja, *The World of the Witches* (Phoenix Press, 1964).

The Divine King: The Slain God

In ancient times, survival based on strength was a very true and experienced reality. In early tribal states, hunters and warriors held a significant place in society. The bravest were honored among the tribe and were considered leaders. In many cases, their well-being affected the tribe's well-being. This is a theme we find present in the King Arthur mythos. Merlin tells Arthur that, if he succeeds, the land will flourish; if he fails, the land will perish. Arthur asks *"why?"* and Merlin replies *"Because you are king!"* Even today, we find that a political leader's ailments are downplayed; they are always recovering well. To understand this intimate relationship, we must look at certain aspects and connections. For as Merlin tells Arthur, *"you are the Land, and the Land is you,"* let us journey back to the past to uncover these roots.

Before humans learned to farm and herd, the hunt was essential to life. Without successful hunters, the clans would perish. Hunting was dangerous; early weapons required the Hunters to be close to the prey, and injuries were common.

Many hunters lost their lives or were permanently injured during hunts. In time, the hunter became the warrior, risking his life for the sake of his tribe. The needs of the tribe, whether for food or defense, required sending out the best the tribe had to offer: hunter or warrior.

In time, this concept formed along with humankind's religious consciousness. The concept of deity and its role in life and death began to form into religious dogma and ritual. Eventually, the idea arose of sending the best of the tribe directly to the gods to secure favors. Some believe this was the birth of human sacrifice. Those who went willingly were believed to become gods themselves. Offerings were nothing new, many times food, flowers, or game, laid out before the gods. To offer one of your own was considered the highest offering the tribe could make. Among human offerings, the sacrifice of a willing human was the height of all possibilities. Surely, it was believed the gods would grant the tribe anything if someone willingly laid down their life.

In his book, *Western Inner Workings*, William Gray addresses many aspects of this cult theme. One of these has to do with bloodlines. Here, he writes: *"Something drove them toward Deities not from fear or for seeking favors, but because they sensed a degree of affinity between themselves and the invisible Immortals. In a remote way they realized they were distantly related to those Gods and wanted to improve that relationship. This trait in specific members of the human race shows some evidence of genetic lines leading back to the 'Old Blood' which originated from outside this Earth altogether."* [59]

Mr. Gray goes on to argue how rulers were sacrificed as the best of the Clan and how ancestry was an important consideration. The rules of ancient Rome and Egypt were considered to descendants of the gods or the gods themselves.

In the chapter "The Cult of Kingship," Gray gives an account of how the blood and flesh were distributed among the clan and into the land. Body parts were buried in cultivated fields to ensure the harvest. He writes: *"They gave their late leader the most honorable*

---

59 William Gray, *Western Inner Workings* (S. Weiser, 1983).

The Divine King: The Slain God

burial of all–in their own stomachs."[60] (All of this can also be found in Christian mythology.) After these practices ended, Mr. Gray notes that the custom remained to burn them in a funeral pyre.

Blood lines are still very important among hereditary Witch families. Witch blood (or being "of the blood," as it is called) is essential to passing on the Craft secrets. In the Old Country, most families will not even discuss the Craft with unrelated Witches. This is one of the most difficult obstacles in trying to teach and maintain the true Old Religion. Guarding family secrets is integral to your upbringing and understanding the self. I still have a problem overcoming this, even with the closest of my initiate friends.

In the Divine King and Slain God mythos, sacrifice is only part of the story. To sacrifice is to send your best, but what about their return? In the Craft, we find a passage which reads: *"...and you must meet, know, remember, and love them again."* Rituals were designed to rebirth these slain gods, and blood lines were carefully traced. Special maidens were prepared to bring about the birth, usually virgins who were artificially inseminated, so that no human male was known to be the father.

As human consciousness matured and evolved, animals replaced humans as scapegoats in ritual sacrifice, and eventually plants replaced animals. Ritual sacrifice is the origin of cakes and wine in Craft rituals, mirroring the custom of eating deity in the flesh and blood. Although the meaning and preparation have been lost to most "reconstructed" systems, they have still been preserved by hereditary traditions such as the Aridian.

In the Ancient Tradition, it was through the body and blood of the Slain God that the people were united with deity. This mirrors the Christian rite of Holy Communion or the Eucharist.

---

60 Ibid.

At the Last Supper, Jesus declares to his followers that the bread and wine were his body and blood. He then declares that he will lay down his life for his people and bids them to eat of his flesh and drink of his blood (the bread and the wine).

Blood was believed to contain the essence of the life force. The death of the king freed the sacred inner spirit, renewed the kingdom through his energy, and by the distribution of his flesh and blood (in the people and the land), heaven and earth were united. Remnants of these practices can still be clearly seen in the Old Religion, although they are veiled and highly symbolic. The Slain Divine King appears in various aspects throughout the ages. His image can be seen in Jack-in-the-Green, the Hooded Man, the Green Man, and even the Hanged Man of the Tarot. He is the Lord of Vegetation, the Harvest, and, in his wild (or free) aspect, he is Lord of the Forest. He does not take the place of the Earth Mother, nor does he usurp her power; instead, he is her complement and consort.

The Green Man image probably best represents the Slain God. He is the Spirit of the Land, manifesting in all plant forms. He is the procreative power, the Seed of Life. His face is obscured within the foliage, but he is always watching. The Green Man signifies the relationship between humanity and Nature. Author William Anderson, in his book *Green Man*, writes: *"He sums up in himself the union that ought to be maintained between humanity and Nature. In himself he is a symbol of hope: he affirms that the wisdom of man can be allied to the instinctive and emotional forces of Nature."* [61]

---

61 William Anderson, *Green Man: The Archetype of Our Oneness with Earth* (HarperCollins, 1990).

The Divine King: The Slain God

In essence, he is our bridge between the worlds, one with Heaven and Earth. To be one with him is to be united with the Source of All Things.

Aradia and the Witches

In 1880, Charles Leland settled in Florence, Italy. He was founder of The Gypsy Lore Society and a member of the Congress of Folklore Society in London. During his lifetime, he wrote several books on Italian folklore. During his stay in Florence in 1886, Leland met an Italian woman by the name of Maddalena. She was a fortuneteller and claimed to belong to a society of Witches. It was from this time forward that Leland began to research the Old Religion of Witchcraft in Italy.

In 1888, Charles Leland wrote: *"There are many people in Italy, and I have met such, who, while knowing nothing about Diana as a Roman Goddess, are quite familiar with her as Queen of the Witches."*

Leland pressed Maddalena for material for his research, and had written a book titled *Aradia: the Gospel of the Witches* in 1899. Leland's book brings forth many questions. Was there an older, non-distorted version of the material? Was Aradia purely myth, or was there some foundation for the whole story? Who was Aradia? In Leland's book, she is the daughter of the Roman deities known as Diana (Goddess of the Moon) and Lucifer (God of Light). To some Witches, she was an avatar who brought about the revival of the Old Religion during the mid-fourteenth century. Is there any evidence of such a revival or of a person named Aradia?

Raven's Call

In 1508, the Italian inquisitor Bernardo Rategno (having studied Witch trial records preserved in the archives of the Inquisition at Como) wrote a text called the *Tractatus de Strigibus*. In this text, he states that the "Witches' sect" expanded rapidly 150 years earlier. This would place the expansion around 1350, which is the mid-fourteenth century. What caused this to happen? The answer may lay hidden in the Legend of *La Pellegrina della Casa al Vento* (The Female Pilgrim of the House of the Wind). This legend appears in Leland's research material, and was even then considered a very old legend. According to this story, there was a young woman from the town of Volterra, who *"traveled far and wide, teaching and preaching the religion of old times, the religion of Diana, the Queen of the Fairies and of the Moon, the Goddess of the poor and the oppressed."*[62] Leland goes on to say, *"And the fame of her wisdom and beauty went forth over all the land, and people worshipped her, calling her La Bella Pellegrina."*[63] Perhaps this legend preserves the memory of Aradia in the fourteenth century.

It is difficult to apply all of Leland's collected myths into a cohesive story. Through the ages, stories change in the retelling, and often take on contemporary aspects as they are recounted. In the Aridian Tradition, it is not Leland's accounts which form our beliefs about Aradia. Our teachings have come to us from the oral tradition and inner court writings of the Triad Clans of Italy. We refer to Aradia as the Holy Strega and honor her memory, but we do not worship her. As to whether she ever really existed, and whether our material comes from the fourteenth century, we find the teachings more important than their origins. I do believe

---

62   Charles Godfrey Leland, "The House of the Wind" in *Aradia: Gospel of the Witches* (David Nutt, 1899). https://sacred-texts.com/pag/aradia/ara13.htm.
63   Ibid.

Aradia and the Witches

that she actually lived and taught according to the Tradition. I also believe that her teachings were passed on through the centuries and have come down to us through an unbroken line. It is important to believe in such things. What is life without magick, myth, and dreams? The very existence of Witches today is a testimony to the survival of things unlikely.

According to our writings, Aradia formed covens (called groves) in central Italy during the fourteenth century. She taught them the old pre-Christian religion of Nature worship and magick, but above all, Aradia taught a spirituality. Beyond this, she gave hope to peasants whose lives were made miserable in service to the wealthy. She taught them personal power and personal value in an age where the Church taught them shame, sin, and servitude. Aradia returned their Pagan heritage to these people, a heritage which was preserved in secret by courageous priests and priestesses of the Old Religion. When Aradia began her teaching, she took the name of an ancient Goddess *(Ara:* fertile earth; *dia:* goddess), who was prophesied to return after the collapse of the matriarchal system, which predated the Christian Era. As covens spread and time passed, some people began to think of Aradia as a goddess, which probably explains why some traditions use Aradia as a Goddess name. It is interesting to note, however, that Carlo Ginzburg in his book *Ecstasies: Deciphering the Witches' Sabbath* tells of a Goddess named "Irodeasa" or "Arada," who was a nocturnal deity. He goes on to associate her with Herodias and Diana.

Aradia taught harmony with Nature and directed her followers to merge with Nature through seasonal rites and ritual observation of the Full Moon. She left her Witches with a complete body of teachings to empower and give insight into a spiritual life. Through religious and spiritual participation, Aradia promised the bestowment of certain gifts.

With a list of these gifts, I shall close this article:

1. To bring success in love
2. To bless and consecrate
3. To speak with spirits
4. To know of hidden things
5. To call forth spirits
6. To know the voice of the wind
7. To possess the knowledge of changing forms
8. To possess the knowledge of divination
9. To know secret signs
10. To cure disease
11. To bring forth beauty
12. To have power over wild beasts
13. To know the secrets of the hands

The Spirit Flame

In the Aridian System, the focal point of the altar is called the Spirit Flame. A bowl is placed upon the center of the altar and filled with a special liquid, which produces a blue flame. The appearance of the blue flame represents the presence of Divinity within the ritual setting. The use of fire as a sacred symbol is one of the most ancient of practices.

In ancient times, fire was a mysterious force. It provided warmth and protection, and was an extremely valuable possession. When people lived in villages and towns, crude lamps were used to provide light. Fuel for these lamps was expensive and therefore had to be used sparingly. Light was only present at night for short periods and was a time for family gathering. Today, with the convenience of modern lighting, it is difficult to appreciate how precious light (and heat) can really be. In time, light became a symbol of all that was positive in human life.

Aradia associated the flame as the soul of the Old Religion. Among her followers, the Spirit Flame became a symbol of the Old Ways. Even today, its symbol appears as a sacred sign of our religion. It is an essential part of setting up the altar, and prescribed gestures and words of evocation are used to empower it as a vessel for divine presence. Traditionally, the bowl, which will bear the flame, is placed upon the pentacle. The four Elemental tools are then placed at each of the cardinal positions around the bowl. The altar candles, which represent the God and Goddess, are set to the far left and right corners of the altar. Together with the Spirit Flame, they will form a triangle of light.

If you are interested in getting an idea of what the Spirit Flame is like, try the following: Obtain some good quality cologne (or Strega Liquor) and pour it in a small bottle, preferably made of green glass. Set it out under the Full Moon for several hours (three is fine). Be sure that the bottle is well-sealed. When you bring it in, pour out that which you will use into a small bowl, filling it about halfway. Extinguish all lights, then trace a crescent over the fluid with your ritual knife, while saying:

*"In the name of Tana,
and by this sacred sign,
be thy essence of magick!"*

Now the fluid is ready to ignite. When you light it, say:

*"I call now upon the Highest of All and pray Thee impart
Thy essence into this most sacred flame!"*

A beautiful blue flame will gently appear and dance upon the surface of the liquid. Now simply sit and look upon the flame. Do not extinguish it, but allow it to go out on its own.

The Spirit Flame

We consider the flame to be sacred and we use it to bless objects, empower tools, and create sacred space. Feel free to experiment with it, but remember to treat it with respect.

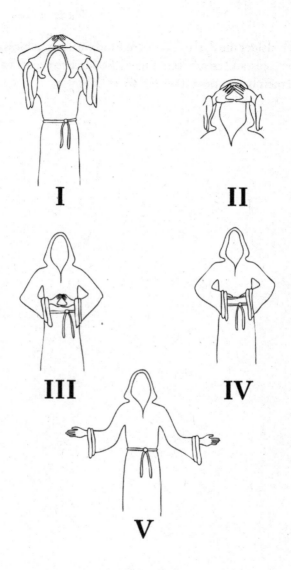

Rite of Union Postures

The Rite of Union

This rite is performed to the sunrise in adoration of the God (through observance of his symbol) and to the Full Moon in adoration to the Goddess (through observance of her symbol). It may also be done at any other time that feels appropriate.

Standing or kneeling before the light (or symbol), raise hands as shown in the first position, saying:

"Hail and adoration unto Thee, O' Source of All Enlightenment. I pray Thee impart to me Thy Illumination."

Lower arms to the second position, saying:

"And enlighten my mind that I may perceive more clearly all things in which I endeavor."

Lower arms to the third position, saying:

"And illuminate my soul, imparting Thy essence of Purity."

Raven's Call

Lower arms to the fourth and fifth position, saying:

"I reveal my Inner Self to Thee and ask that all be cleansed and purified within."

The Nanta Bag

The nanta bag is a very old tool, appearing in various forms as it is traced back through the ages. The form in which we have it today comes to us from fifteenth-century Italy. Its purpose is twofold: first, it is designed to keep its wearer in harmony with the forces of Nature. Second, it serves as a carrier for the Tools of the Art, so that a Witch can perform their magick anywhere. The original followers of Aradia carried them as they traveled from village to village, and they soon became a symbol of the priesthood of the Old Religion.

Within these bags were miniature representations of the ritual tools, along with Elemental symbols and objects of personal power. Typically, the bag would contain a thimble (chalice), a needle or pin (ritual blade), a coin (pentacle), and a twig (wand). Also included would be a stone (Earth), a feather (Air), a flint stone or match (Fire), and a shell or vial of liquid (Water). Finally, the bag would contain a symbol for the God and Goddess, along with objects of personal meaning. If someone was given a small token by one whose power they respected, then this also would be added to the nanta bag.

Raven's Call

The principle of contagion magick was the foundation for empowering the bag. Objects absorb power and have an energy field around them. When one object is placed into contact with another, they are joined and influence one another. The nanta bag in turn influences the person who carries it (in direct proportion to the items it contains). The following is a basic example of a functional nanta bag:

- 1 small stone, smooth and rounded
- 1 small feather, blue or very light in color
- 1 small portion of ash (wood or coal)
- 1 small vessel of pure water
- 1 small coin with a five-pointed star etched upon it
- 1 small twig (fruit or nutwood)
- 1 pin with a black head (or a needle)
- 1 thimble
- Portion of incense
- 2 small white candles
- 1 piece of marking chalk
- 1 measure of cord (nine feet)
- 1 small finger-sized bowl (cup or dish)
- Symbol of the God (an acorn, small pinecone, piece of horn, etc.)
- Symbol of the Goddess (a seashell, string of beads, nutshell, etc.)
- 1 personal power object (a lucky piece, a crystal, etc.)
- A portion of salt
- A small vessel of anointing oil

Collect these items and make a bag of leather or cloth large enough to contain them. You may wish to add some healing herbs or other desired items. The first four items are to be gathered in a manner which brings you into contact with the Element represented. Take the completed bag and consecrate it in the manner of the altar tools, charging by the Elements and Gesture of Power. Then, say over the completed bag:

> *"O' Great Nanta bag, be thou a natural focus*
> *and a bridge to power.*
> *I am linked to thee and thou art linked to Nature.*
> *We are one from three.*
> *We are the Triangle manifest.*
> *In the names of Tana and Tanus,*
> *so be it."*

The Fava Bean

The fava bean has long been associated with the mystery tradition of Southern European Witchcraft. The ancient Romans grew fava plants in their cemeteries and served the beans as the most sacred dish at funeral banquets. During the nine-day passage between winter and spring (the Parentalia in February), the Romans honored their dead ancestors with offerings of fava beans, milk, and honey. The Greeks viewed the black spot on the petals of fava plants as the symbol of death and believed that their hollow stems penetrated down into the Underworld. It was from this belief that the fava was thought to connect the living and the dead.

In the Italian Witchcraft traditions, fava beans are prepared on October 31st as offerings to the souls and spirits that dwell in the otherworld. Bowls of fava bean soup are placed outside at midnight and are buried after sunrise on November 1st. At certain celebrations, a fava bean is baked into one of the ritual cakes. The finding of the bean can signify several different things depending upon the season. In some cases, a temporary title is bestowed (or office is held). Fava beans are also dried and placed upon the Lares shrine within the family home. This serves as a connection with those who have passed into the otherworld, linking one back through the ages to the first of the Witch Clans.

In the tenth century, Christian monks gathered at the Abbey of Cluny to celebrate All Souls Day. Here, they were confronted with the Pagan fava bean custom. Being masters of conversion, they boiled huge batches of fava beans and offered them up for the souls of the dead. Tubs of favas were placed on the streetcorners, and everyone (especially the poor) came to take their fill. It wasn't until the fifteenth century that the Church officially recognized the festival as a day dedicated to the dead, naming it *Ognissanti* (All Saints Day).

Fava plants are cold tolerant and can withstand acidic soil. They are excellent at drawing excess moisture from the ground and can fix up to 150lbs of nitrogen per acre. Favas were the only beans known to Europeans prior to the colonization of the Americas. They are a type of vetch rather than belonging to the *Phaseolus* genus of beans. They grow well in areas of mild winter and should be planted in the fall when the soil is between sixty to eighty-five degrees.

The beans grown in large, fat pods, and resemble lima beans, but are much bigger. Once planted, the fava beans are 85 days to harvest. When viewed vertically from the side, the bean resembles human male genitalia. When viewed on the bottom (dark end), it looks very much like human female genitalia. Fava beans usually appear in western markets in early spring and are often plentiful between June through September.

Bibliography

Anderson, William. *Green Man: The Archetype of Our Oneness with Earth*. HarperCollins, 1990.

Baroja, Julio C. *The World of the Witches*. Phoenix Press, 2001.

Bonnefoy, Yves. *Roman and European Mythologies*. University of Chicago Press, 1992.

Borgeaud, Phillip. *The Cult of Pan in Ancient Greece*. University of Chicago Press, 1988.

Campbell, Joseph. *The Hero with a Thousand Faces*. New World Library, 2008.

Cooper, J. C.. *The Aquarian Dictionary of Festivals*. Wildside Press, LLC, 1990.

Dumezil, George. *Archaic Roman Religion*. John Hopkins University Press, 1996.

Eliade, Mircea. *Occultism, Witchcraft, and Cultural Fashions: Essays in Comparative Religion*. University of Chicago Press, 2012.

Falassi, Alessandro. *Folklore by the Fireside: Text and Context of the Tuscan Veglia*. University of Texas Press, 1980.

Farrar, Janet and Stewart. *Eight Sabbats for Witches*. Robert Hale, 1981.

Field, Carol. *Celebrating Italy: The Tastes and Traditions of Italy Through Its Feasts, Festivals & Sumptuous Foods*. HarperCollins, 1997.

Frazer, James. *The Golden Bough: A Study in Magic and Religion.* Oxford University Press, 1998.

Gimbutas, Marija. *The Goddesses and Gods of Old Europe.* University of California Press, 2007.

Ginzburg, Carlo. *The Night Battles: Witchcraft & Agrarian Cults in the Sixteenth & Seventeenth Centuries.* Routledge & Kegan Paul, 1983.

Gray, William. *Western Inner Workings.* S. Weiser, 1983.

Hazlitt, W. C.. *Dictionary of Faiths & Folklore.* Bracken Books, 1995.

Kerenyi, Carl. *Dionysos: Archetypal Image of Indestructible Life.* Princeton University Press, 1976.

Kingsley, Peter. *Ancient Philosophy, Mystery, and Magic.* Oxford University Press, 1995.

Leland, Charles. "Aradia." *Aradia, Gospel of the Witches*, Sacred Texts, sacred-texts.com/pag/aradia/index.htm. Accessed 10 Oct. 2024.

—. *Etruscan Magic & Occult Remedies.* University Books, 1963.

—. *Etruscan Roman Remains in Popular Tradition.* Charles Scribner's Sons, 1892.

—. *Gypsy Sorcery and Fortune Telling.* Charles Scribner's Sons, 1891.

—. *Legends of Florence: Collected from the People.* David Nutt, 1895.

MacKillop, James. *Dictionary of Celtic Mythology.* Oxford University Press, 1998.